The North Light

·A·R·T·
COMPETITION HANDBOOK

John M. Angelini, AWS

North Light Publishers

The cover painting, *Mining Town*, is used with permission of the artist, LaVere Hutchings.

Published by North Light, an imprint of Writer's Digest Books, 9933 Alliance Road, Cincinnati, Ohio 45242.

Manufactured in U.S.A.
First Printing 1986

Library of Congress Cataloging-in-Publication Data

Angelini, John M., 1921-
The North Light art competition handbook.
Includes index.
1. Art—Competitions—Handbooks, manuals, etc. I. Title.
N393.A54 1986 706'.8'8 85-29793
ISBN 0-89134-130-7

Design by Carol Buchanan

Acknowledgments

Berkeley Express Company
Butler Institute of American Art
DeLand Museum
Exhibition Planners
Foothills Art Center, Inc.
Graphik Dimensions, Ltd.
House Foreign Affairs Committee, United States Congress
G.M. Irvine
Kentucky Watercolor Society
R.H. Lecznar, Attorney at Law
Pro-Pak, Inc.
Regency Worldwide Packing, Inc.
Ritz Camera Centers
State Farm Insurance Companies
J. Torkelson
United Parcel Service

Contents

To "Lizzy":
confidante, critic, devotee,
and wife.

Foreword

The *North Light Art Competition Handbook* was written in response to artists pleading for answers. Their voices reawakened memories of moments when the competitive system seemed to favor already established artists. The process appeared less than equitable. But I found comfort in knowing that there must be a beginning to all processes and that advancement in any endeavor is a matter of finding answers and taking the initial plunge.

Where were these answers to be found? Certainly not in any comprehensive form. Information was a word-of-mouth process that rendered involvement with the competitive system a hit or miss game.

In spite of these obstacles I tolerated the growing pains and somehow found my way into the competitive system.

Even now—in spite of concerted efforts by both artists and sponsoring art organizations—many aspects of the competitive system are filled with hopes that need mending.

With the system's existing problems in mind it is the objective of *The North Light Art Competition Handbook* to assist all artists in understanding what has been, and what lies ahead. I will share with you whatever wisdom I've grasped over many years of trial and error, success and failure, and attempt to offer a reasonably secure path to follow. But bear in mind that nothing proclaimed is ever *sacrosanct;* that arriving at a given point in what can be a less than complicated competitive process depends on turning an attentive ear besides a strong measure of common sense.

To the often asked question, "Where do I start?" my answer always seemed less than adequate. The question, "What do I send?" was usually greeted with silence since I had no knowledge of the caller's works or creative ability. Without dismissing the plea, I tried to make clear that responsibility for such a decision cannot be shared, that maturity develops with good and bad choices, and that acceptance and rejection often is based less on personal selection than on factors beyond anyone's control.

I remember staring at dozens of paintings standing in my studio, living room, and dining room that seemed to shout: "Pick me!" In desperation I would solicit the help of my wife or children. Once my cat was shoved into the rooms. The first painting *he* sniffed was *my* selection. On several occasions, numbers corresponding to each work were tossed into a paper bag. The method lasted until the first failure, when the cat was again shoved into the room. There were no easy solutions then or now.

Other answers to other questions were treated with patience, sympathy, and a reminder that creativity is its own reward and everything else mere residual benefits. I would remind the questioner that the competitive system grows less frightening with each confrontation and that experience nurtures confidence and artistic maturity promotes a less rigid denial of one's competence.

But, unless we deceive ourselves into believing that competitive exhibiting is simply a matter of numbers in a hat or picking the brains of a nosy cat, be assured the course is puckered with obstacles (all surmountable)—with warning signs (quickly heeded)—with procedures, restrictions, requirements, and limitations (easily followed)—with smiles and tears (hopefully more of the former than the latter), and finally, with someone dedicated to help you every step of the way. That's what this book is all about.

Chapter 1

OPPORTUNITIES

After 30 years of exhibiting I'm still excited by each new opportunity. If I can help you experience the same feeling, then together we will have accomplished our goal. It won't be easy at first. The struggle to succeed is frustrating. Competitions are a gamble. Though your creative ability determines your chances, you may lose unless you follow a step-by-step course of action.

As for where to start, keep in mind that competing at the top, before placing your "bet" against reasonable odds, could discourage you and defeat your goals in spite of your efforts. By all means aim high—but start at the bottom and work your way up. With time, patience and experience, your climb gets easier.

Initially, exhibiting may seem to be a confusing process. It's important to have access to information. Once you know where to look, the process becomes easier. Unfortunately, there's no single publication that covers all competitive exhibitions. The task of compiling accurate data from virtually thousands of art groups is logistically impossible since shows are often subject to scheduling changes.

But there are ways to get information. Scan your local and larger circulation newspapers, most of which list pending art shows far in advance. This lead time gives you ample opportunity to make inquiries by phone or mail.

Check the art store where you buy supplies for posters announcing forthcoming shows. Ask the owner for information. He's likely to be a knowledgeable data bank of the local art scene. His business depends on *your* craft, and exhibiting is an important part.

Some states have nonprofit art federations which publish newsletters to assist exhibiting artists. Your county or state art council is another useful tool for information.

Other sources include art magazines. For a small fee organizations list exhibition data in these magazines.

These listings indicate their various scopes—from statewide to regional to national to international—including how and where to apply.

The following national magazines provide the most comprehensive listings.

American Artist
Subscription Dept.
1 Colour Court
Marion, OH 43305

Artweek
1628 Telegraph Ave.
Oakland, CA 94612

The Artist's Magazine
P.O. Box 1999
Marion, OH 43305

American Artist and *The Artist's Magazine* are published monthly. *Artweek* is published weekly September through May and biweekly June through August. *American Artist's* "Bulletin Board" lists information by state in alphabetical order. *Artweek*'s "Competitions" provides separate categories under international, national, regional, festivals, and miscellaneous headings.

Exhibition Planners, Box 55, Delmar, New York 12054, publishes the *Exhibition Directory* in July, covering approximately 300 regional and national juried art and photographic exhibitions with information on entry dates, media, awards, fees, and methods of delivery.

American Art Directory, published annually by R. R. Bowker Co., 205 East 42nd Street, New York, New York 10017, can be found in the art department reference section of your public library. Available material is given as follows:

1. Every state art council is listed in alphabetical order with its address.

2. National Endowment for the Arts regional

representatives are broken down into seven geographical regions.

3. Newspapers carrying art notices and the names of their art or photography critics are listed alphabetically by state.

4. Scholarships and fellowships are listed alphabetically by state.

American Craft is published bimonthly by the American Craft Council, 401 Park Avenue South, New York, New York 10016. Opportunities presented by "Where to Show" organizations in different states are listed. Crafts find their greatest potential in outdoor art exhibitions and festivals.

These publications do not cover every geographical location. Those that do are available at your state art council, public library, or university art departments. Advance guides provide sufficient information to prepare an annual exhibition schedule. However, keep your plans flexible to allow for unexpected new prospects.

It's time to decide where to start. Opportunities are available at these levels:

1. Local
2. State
3. Regional
4. National
5. International
6. Outdoor
7. Restricted
8. Commercial/Industrial

Each level will be examined thoroughly to help you decide where to begin.

Local

Limited experience makes it advisable to start at the local level. As your competence grows, the experience you gain becomes an invaluable asset. Taking classes and joining art groups are important, because artists are stimulated by each other's works in a group atmosphere. They try harder when faced with someone else's admirable efforts. I'm not implying an atmosphere of sheer competitiveness exists but rather one of influence. Creativity does not flourish in a vacuum. Allow yourself to be inspired by others.

Contact also means keeping abreast of other sources of knowledge. Read. Collect art books or join a library. Art books—texts and illustrations—help to develop your skills.

I recommend paying the fee to join a museum. You will receive a monthly bulletin listing exhibitions, lecture series, acquisitions, field trips, and other information. The Tampa Museum, where I'm a member, is quite diversified. Its exhibitions range from the archaeological to the contemporary. I find this variation more exciting than with some museums that specialize in certain art periods.

Another form of contact is to attend art lectures and demonstrations. Both are often sponsored by museums, art organizations, or private groups interested in expanding cultural influence in the community.

Local groups conduct various types of classes. Some are informal sessions without a teacher, where you can meet with others and work in the medium of your choice. I used to attend a life class at an art center which met every Thursday night. A monitor, not an instructor, hired models, arranged poses, and kept time. Both nonprofessionals and professionals attended. The class included a dentist, a lawyer, and a town water inspector, among others. Other local groups hire instructors. If possible, try several groups to enjoy the benefits of each.

An advantage of a local group is its members' shows, which provide the opportunity to display your work. Little or no fee is charged, and class work is permitted.

Volunteering could provide worthwhile experiences. By becoming a member of an exhibition committee, you'll get an understanding of how an "open" competition works. (An "open" is defined as one or more works to be presented before a hand-picked jury of selection and awards.) The juries are governed by a set of rules and regulations determined by the sponsoring organization.

As a committee person you'll meet the nucleus of the group—those dedicated people working for betterment of the organization. Some of these people may act as judges for members' shows, providing you with firsthand knowledge of how the system works.

Joining a fund-raising committee will help you meet people who are dedicated to the arts. Donated funds help defray mailing expenses and catalog costs, and are necessary for expanded activities. These donations are also used for awards. A donor may specify an award amount in his name and be listed in the exhibition catalog. Membership dues alone rarely support a group.

Consider joining the exhibition reception committee. Serving food and drink is an excellent way to meet fellow artists and patrons. The people you come in contact with can provide important information.

Volunteer to be catalogue chairperson. You'll deal directly with typesetters, photostatters, ink experts, and printers. This knowledge will help when you have your own calling cards, stationery, autobiographical sketches, show brochures, and other printed matter made up.

Best of all, become a member of an organization's board of directors. Learn all there is to know about its operations.

To be involved at the local level prepares you for more ambitious undertakings. Experience spells the difference between knowing and not knowing what happens behind the scene once your piece of art is delivered to a show. This knowledge does not in any way guarantee success but helps you to understand that a jury has complete authority in the selection process and is in no way influenced by the sponsoring organization.

State

The state level of open competitions usually seeks residents and sometimes former residents as well. An organization's prospectus should declare eligibility requirements. However, don't waste time and postage asking for an out-of-state prospectus if you've never lived there.

You may want to confine your exhibiting to state and local shows so hand delivery is possible. Larger states may require a day's drive to and from your destination. In spite of this, it's considerably easier to hand deliver than crate and ship. Some use a reciprocal system: a network of artists taking turns handling delivery and pickup.

Now on to some specifics. Let's say you're a resident of Michigan and read an announcement in the "Bulletin Board" of *American Artist*. This announcement is typical of a show restricted to state artists and is printed *verbatim*. (The numbers are mine and are used for ease of reference.)

1 Michigan, Lansing. "Images of Michigan's Heritage."
2 May 5-Sept. 1, 1984 at Mich. Historical Museum. Open
3 to Mich. artists. Media: 2-dimensional, no photography.
4 Juried by slides. Fee: none. Commission: none. Slides due
5 Jan. 23. $1,200 in purch. awards. Encl. SASE. Write:
6 Michigan Historical Museum, 208 N. Capitol Ave., Lans-
7 ing. MI 48918 or 373-2177.

Line 1 describes the nature of the exhibition, but past experience has shown that subject matter is often treated with leniency. For example, a church that sponsored a religious art show accepted a painting of three peony flowers entitled "The Holy Trinity."

Line 2 is self-explanatory.

Line 3 is quite specific. "Open to Michigan artists" means exactly that. "Media: 2-dimensional" states only framed works for hanging are wanted. Sculpture is unacceptable. "No photography" is also a restriction by the sponsoring organization.

Line 4 is an example of the growing tendency to judge by slides. Actually, this benefits everyone. "Fee: none." is an exception to the rule, since entry fees are usually required. The fee has been waived, because the Michigan Historical Museum is a nonprofit, publicly supported institution. "Commission: none" is another exception. Sales commissions are customary, because the art group performs a sales task similar to a commercial gallery.

Lines 4 and 5 state, "Slides due Jan. 23." Sounds simple, but you could overlook an important consideration. Let's go back to line 2: "May 5-Sept. 1, 1984." From slide submission date, Jan. 23, to opening day, May 5, is a period of over three months. During that time, slides are viewed and paintings selected, followed by deliveries. Until your slide is judged the painting it represents cannot be entered in any other show unless that show ends before the delivery date. If someone suddenly wants to purchase that painting do whatever is necessary to consummate the sale without jeopardizing your integrity.

In most cases the prospective buyer puts the painting on hold with a deposit and waits until the show ends. If your slide is rejected, you have no problem. But what if the slide is accepted? Things become tricky if you win a purchase award (see below). There's only one way to handle such a situation. Spell it out to the buyer and see if he's willing to accept the conditions. If not, ask him to consider one of your other works.

The phrase "1,200 in purch. awards" means awards where you retain possession of your painting will not be presented. Works will be purchased outright to supplement an existing collection. "Encl. SASE," enclose self-addressed, stamped envelope, is another recent development to save costs and expedite the return of jury results and of your slides, if rejected. Since most organizations keep slides of accepted works, I would advise having duplicates made of anything submitted.

Lines 6 and 7 are self-explanatory. A phone number is included for those who may be pressed to meet the due date. Calling could save you several days time.

The foregoing "Bulletin Board" entry is typical. Everything is easy if you follow directions.

Regional

Regional shows are similar to state and local with some exceptions.

A local show entails tagging and delivering your entry. A state competitive show sometimes requests an entry fee and registration card in advance. The advance registration helps an organization predetermine the number of entries and thus decide the number of volunteers needed to cart and stack entries. In state and local shows the actual work—rather than a slide—is judged.

Regionals are a different situation. The term regional suggests an area larger than a state. As a potential participant, consider the size of the regional areas; you must be aware of the involvement both for the organization and for you, the artist. The recent method changes mentioned earlier have simplified procedures to some extent. At one time, the artist crated the work and shipped it off. Crates were stored until the selection jury made its decision. Rejects were recrated and returned. Accepted works were shipped back in the original containers when the show ended. The major drawback to this method was the expense, especially to the rejected artist. Many artists refused to submit under such conditions. Art organizations were just as dissatisfied. The involvement of uncrating and crating hundreds of rejected art pieces seemed unnecessary. This forced many organizations to change their policies. With everyone's interest in mind, the present method of slide submission was established and has gained much favor.

Now, most regionals are prejudged. The time period between receiving your prospectus and the submission date is ample enough to photograph your work and process your slides. Always keep some extras available to avoid missing a sudden exhibition opportunity. The importance of color fidelity and sharpness cannot be overstressed. Beautiful works have been rejected because of inferior slide-color quality.

Once jury selections are made, you will be notified by mail. It's up to you to crate and ship your work properly. Give yourself plenty of delivery time leeway. If your entry arrives late, it may be automatically rejected. At this stage of the process, accepted paintings are judged again for awards.

A major drawback to some regionals is media restriction. For example, many totally forbid sculpture. Weight, bulk, damage potential, and shipping costs often prevent sculptors themselves from submitting. There are some exceptions where organizations permit hand delivery.

Distance is another consideration with regionals. You may have to travel far to see your artwork displayed, meet your peers, and enjoy the excitement of an opening night reception. Many artists plan vacations around such events, exploring and photographing these new environments for reference material. The experience could be rewarding and helpful in your work.

National

National shows are the most prestigious and competitive, and certainly the most rewarding. Acceptance in a national show provides an important clue to your development potential—not that a rejection automatically implies creative stagnation. Few artists enjoy 100 percent acceptance. A major problem is a question of simple mathematics—the number of accepted works versus the number of entries. I cannot repeat often enough that national shows attract artists from all fifty states. Obviously this reduces anyone's chances but the challenge is a thrilling experience.

Understanding the jury process involved in a national show is important to you. You'll see why acceptance or rejection doesn't mean you're a creative hero or an "automatic" victim. It's all part of a larger picture.

A jury works in different ways, depending upon the various organizational policies involved. I don't mean that the sponsoring group necessarily has a hand in the selection process. Some may predesignate the show's personality. Usually, a jury is given a set of conditions for selecting the show. A typical jury question may be, "How many pieces can you hang?" The reply could be a specific number or, "Only the very best, regardless of numbers." Faced with this, a jury may scan all entries quickly to establish overall quality. Superior work will *sing out* and almost always be selected immediately. The rest will be viewed and reviewed until the process is complete.

Jury processes vary dramatically. No two are ever completely alike except possibly within the structure of a specific organization. One in particular uses seven judges and relies on unanimous agreement for acceptance. In some cases, but not many, a lone judge with a particular discipline, be it *avant-garde* or realism, is selected to assemble an exhibition based on his forte. An organization may provide a clue to its intention by profiling the judge's background in its prospectus. His "charge" may be to select an all abstract and semi-abstract show. Or the reverse may be true, as in the Professional Artists League exhibitions, when it states unequivocally its preferences in black and white: "Only realistic art accepted."

National shows are always judged by slides. I repeat myself to etch *slide* into your mind. Learn to consider *it* as your entry.

However, the Gulf Coast Art Center of Belleair, Florida prejudges by slides but reserves the right to make a final judgment based on a review of the actual work.

People and space requirements of hand delivered and shipped works would have ultimately doomed the national shows. The one noteworthy exception is the miniature art show. These organizations restrict size to 8x10 maximum, including frame, and find it more convenient to judge directly than by conducting the process twice.

Another exception is the New York Pen and Brush Club's annual open sculpture exhibition where 8x10 black-and-white photos are preferred to color slides.

Some organizations which deal in all-media print exhibitions accept unframed matted works in specific sizes. These pieces are displayed under glass. Again, in this case, packing and shipping costs are reasonable because of size and weight.

Today art organizations flourish at every level, making selectivity a number-one priority. Choose your opportunities wisely. Selectivity is particularly important when one or more exhibitions overlap. With this in mind you must keep an accurate ledger, listing delivery, reception, rejection, and pick-up dates, as well as other information. An up-to-date log at your fingertips lets you make wise entry decisions without conflict.

Suppose you have selected a vintage painting. Before submitting your slide, double-check your prospectus. You may read such statements as: "Only works executed since 1981 are eligible," or "Any work may not be more than five years old." The intention is not to deny the artistic merit of an older work. Organizations maintain a keener interest in your latest endeavors. They are interested in seeking new and talented potential members. Organizations prefer to see what you are doing now. Submit your very latest and best; do not submit the same painting again to the same show—ever!

Another interesting aspect worth mentioning are the travel shows sponsored by several organizations. The San Diego Watercolor Society awards juror selects thirty paintings for a year-long nationwide circuit. The American Watercolor Society selects fifty for the same purpose and insures each painting for $1,000. All exhibitors are eligible for this honor. The SDWS tour participants pay an additional $30 fee, a small sum considering the excellent exposure in various cultural institutions across the United States. When a painting is sold the artist is expected to replace it by sending another to the next tour stop. Tours of this nature are often arranged by William D. Gorman and Jan Gorman of the Old Bergen Art Guild in Bayonne, New Jersey.

International

At one time international shows were restricted to invited artists only. Major art capitals of the world mounted exhibitions that competed against one another. The controversies surrounding their invitational policies threatened the continuation of these exhibitions. Those artists not invited were among those who questioned the invitational criteria.

Today, some American organizations use the word "international" in an exhibition's title more for prestige than as a serious attempt to attract overseas artists. One particular West Coast organization's use of "international" implies anyone in the world may submit, but its prospectus does not include information regarding customs regulations. Under certain conditions, according to the United States Customs Service, merchandise and artworks may be entered duty free via "Temporary Importation under Bond" (TIB) procedures. Those ready to consider exhibiting internationally should contact the nearest United States Customs Service office for their book of regulations. Or write to:

Department of the Treasury
United States Customs Service
Washington, DC 20229

Most of the groups involved in miniature art—a movement now proliferating in many states—sponsor international art shows. Florida hosts a competition which usually attracts about 1,200 entries from all over the world. In 1984, 700 in all media were accepted, with 44 awards presented in 20 categories.

The ability to hang so many works is based on size. Sculpture is also subject to size restrictions. These limitations facilitate shipping from anywhere at minimal expense. Miniature painting is not only a worthwhile art experiment, but an exhibition of it in vast numbers is a most unusual experience.

Vanity shows, a new international attraction, appeal to an artist's vanity rather than to his creative ability. Inclusion in these shows has little to do with your stature as an artist and may impede your artistic development. When noted on your resume, these credentials may raise questions about your integrity and creative ability.

I recently received a prospectus for an international show sponsored by *Le Salon des Nations a Paris*. Actually, I received two, both addressed to me as "Dear Artist" indicating that less attention was paid to me as an artist than as someone whose "availability" might have been noted from membership lists of any number of organizations I belong to. I studied the prospectus thoroughly. (The direct quotes are in italics and numbered, and my analysis follows where indicated.)

1. *It is exclusively reserved for independent artists, and we are very pleased to invite you to take part in this event . . .*

2. *The paintings, sculptures, drawings, watercolors, pastels, photographs, and tapestries which have been shown have introduced artists of all nationalities to new outlets and profitable connections sometimes from totally unexpected quarters.*

3. *There will be ten nominations as follows:*
The Gold Medal, 1st prize with award.

The Silver Medal.
The Bronze Medal.
Seven Accessits (honorable mentions)

Sound impressive? By contrast, the American Watercolor Society awards $15,000 in cash and nine medals. The Allied Artists of America, Inc. awards $12,000 in cash and eight medals. The Audubon Artists, Inc. awards $7,300 in cash and ten medals. These representative examples are national shows, all charging a $10 entry fee.

4. *Your participation will involve seven of your most characteristic works chosen by you.*

5. *The history of your work and its value will be featured in the S.D.N.P. catalogues which we shall publish and distribute free to visitors to the exhibition.*

6. *We shall have 50 invitations printed with your name, which we will send you.*

Why would you need fifty invitations to an exhibition in Paris?

7. *If you wish to attend the opening day of the Exhibition, the Salon will give you a free room for one night, in the heart of Paris, at the very fine Hotel Holiday Inn (4 stars) 10 place de la Republique, Paris 75011. You will be given a very warm welcome.*

Sounds generous. Consider the plane fare during the busy travel season, particularly if you live on the West Coast. Who would fly to Paris just for an opening reception? Arranging a charter flight, which often includes your hotel and some meals, would be a smarter move.

8. *Conditions of entry are as follows: The Salon*

des Nations will take 15% commission of each work sold.

A participation fee, which includes payment for organizing expenses of the Salon des Nations totalling $990 is payable as follows: $190 reservation fee to be sent with your entry form. $350 Before April 15, 1984, and the rest ($450) before May 20, 1984.

This is clear enough. In view of your other costs, the sum requires sober thought.

9. *I attach to the present entry form two identity photos of myself and two black and white photographs (sized 13 x 18 cm) of the work to be reproduced in the catalogue.*

Good photography requires some expertise. Either do it yourself or have it done commercially. For better quality, you may want to consider using a commercial photographer in spite of the additional cost.

10. *Categories and formats . . . all formats accepted up to 100 × 81 cm (39″ × 32″ approx.) or equivalent area.*

11. *For tapestries, sculptures, and other works with dimensions which are unusual or larger than the stated size, the artist must consult the organizers of the Salon des Nations before sending in his entry form. Such consultation will be by letter and will include all technical data relevant to the collection he wishes to exhibit. The Salon des Nations will reply by letter.*

12. *Transport and Customs: The Salon des Nations at its expense and under its exclusive responsibility, and under the conditions and within the limits set forth below, will undertake the shipment of the works, round trip, from Long Island, N.Y., to Paris and from Paris to*

Long Island, N.Y. as well as being responsible for all customs formalities and declarations pertaining to them. The artist is formally restrained from arranging the transport of his works without the express consent of the Salon des Nations. The Salon des Nations will be free of all responsibility for an inward and outward transport which is arranged by any other party, and can in no case allow any reduction in the organizing expense due from the artist by reason of his participation in the exhibition.

The instructions are worthy of serious thought. Since the *Salon des Nations* pays shipping costs from Long Island, New York to Paris and back, you must pay to ship your works to and from Long Island. This expense cannot be estimated since many factors apply: size and weight of your shipment, point of origin, carrier (i.e., UPS, United States Postal Service, bus, or air freight), each with its restrictions regarding size and item packaged. Later we will discuss packing and shipping within the U.S. continental limits.

13. *Delivery and collection of exhibits . . . When the exhibition is over, the works which have not been sold will be collected by the artist or his agents from the place where he delivered them initially (Long Island, N.Y.) at the dates and times communicated to him in writing as soon as the customs formalities have been completed. In all cases, the artist must take possession of his works within a maximum of fifteen days from his receipt of the letter informing him of the return of his exhibits. After this period neither the depository nor the Salon des Nations can be held responsible for any damage or loss, however caused.*

How do you arrange to have your works returned from Long Island? Artists within driving range have no problem. For those from greater distances, you can travel to and from Long Island to cart your works or designate an agent to arrange the shipment. But who? Unless you have a friend within the area willing to accept the responsibility, you will require a commercial art carrier to do it for you.

14. *Packing . . . The artist expressly undertakes to use only a wood or cardboard packing case with an easily opened top if the collection is composed of paintings, drawings, etc. . . . The depth of the package shall not exceed 60 cm (24") . . . a single packing case must hold the seven works. The artist shall stick a colored label duly filled in on his package. This label will be sent after acceptance of his entry by the Salon Des Nations.*

Packing seven works for overseas shipment is quite an undertaking. A commercial crater is recommended.

15. *Photographs for Transport Formalities: The artist must send four black and white or color photographs of each work exhibited: polaroid photographs are sufficient . . .*

We are expected to submit 28 black-and-white prints. Polaroid shots are acceptable, and you will need about four packs of film, at an average of $8 to $9 each. These prints merely represent identification of your works for customs.

16. *Insurance: The Salon des Nations expressly undertakes to maintain all contracts of insurance to cover its responsibility in case of fire, water damage, or theft of the works entrusted to it. The Salon des Nations will be responsible to the artist for works entrusted to it from the day of their reception at the exhibition premises to the day of their return to the transporters for return to Long Island, N.Y. The responsibility of the Salon des Nations is confined to loss or damage by fire, water, or theft while the works are on the exhibition premises.*

The *Salon des Nations's* responsibility begins only while the artwork is on their premises. Under no circumstances should artwork be shipped to the *Salon* and back without adequate insurance.

17. *Commitment: In the event that the present agreement cannot be fulfilled for any reason attributable to the Salon des Nations, the latter will reimburse the artist for all sums received, and in the event will make it the personal responsibility of the Salon des Nations to return all works received to the artist, all costs to be borne by the Salon. The artist expressly agrees that he shall not claim any interests or damages whatsoever by way of material or other damages as a result of this cancellation. In the event that the present agreement cannot be fulfilled for any reason attributable to the artist, or for reasons of force majeure, the entire sum remains the property of the Salon des Nations without recourse. The Salon cannot be held responsible for any fault or difficulty arising from any act of the transporter or his agents which may prevent the exhibition from taking place between the dates indicated in the Entry Form returned by the artist. Any such situation will give no right of reimbursement, and in such case it will be the responsibility of the Salon to arrange new dates for the exhibition and to organize it according to the details given in these regulations.*

The commitment, as stated by the *Salon des Nations,* is clear. Some further observations:

a. In the event of cancellation, the *Salon* will return your fee but is not responsible for expenses involved in crating, shipping, and insurance from point of origin to Paris.

b. Conversely, if you are forced to cancel, your fee is lost. The term "force majeure" means an inevitable, accidental, or extraordinary episode, which cannot be foreseen and guarded against, resulting from storms, lightning, etc. Whether this includes illness, accident, or death is questionable.

c. The *Salon des Nations* will not be held responsible if the transporter does not deliver on time.

d. Liability on the *Salon's* or the artist's part may be open to legal interpretation.

The prospectus for this particular international exhibition presents several reasons for reflection: What purpose is served in entering? Is the expense worth the effort, and does it establish your reputation as an international artist? Absolutely not! Only a *bona fide* international invitational does that. Furthermore, vanity shows are a deception and contradict your legitimate standing in the art world.

An artist entered the *Salon des Nations* exhibition and in one grandiose gesture submitted a news release to the local section of a well-known newspaper. It was printed. The publicity release stated, in essence, that the artist was invited to exhibit in Paris without explaining the circumstances. What it neglected to include was the large number of artists "invited" and that anyone willing to spend a great deal of money was eligible, and that quality was not, apparently, a consideration. This is deceptive and contrary to the thrust of any news release (later described in detail).

After having spent so much time with *Le Salon's* prospectus, you should know that it was revealed by the Cultural Affairs Office of the French Embassy that *Le Salon des Nations,* 27 Rue Taine, Paris, France does not exist at that address!

I also learned that the *affaire Le Salon* was under investigation by the House Foreign Affairs Committee in Washington, D.C. I made inquiries and received the following letter:

Congress of the United States
Committee on Foreign Affairs
House of Representatives
Washington, D.C. 20515

August 29, 1984

Mr. John M. Angelini
12603 Pecan Tree Drive
Hudson, Florida 33562

Dear Mr. Angelini:

Thank you for your recent letter concerning Le Salon Des Nations in Paris. I appreciate your interest in this matter.

Congressman William Broomfield of Michigan asked me to look into a number of allegations made by American artists who participated in earlier art exhibits sponsored by the same group which sponsors Le Salon Des Nations.

In the 1975 American Artists Exhibition in Paris, many of the art works were not returned to their owners in the United States and others were badly damaged. Contrary to the claims of the organizers, the art works had not been insured. Although the sponsors of past exhibitions claimed that they had insured the art works, we have been unable to verify that the art was, in fact, insured by Lloyds of London.

The organizers also make a number of claims in their literature about the exhibits which are misleading, and only partially true. I have also been in touch with INTERPOL regarding the activities and affiliations of the groups sponsoring the exhibitions.

Various European art groups that participated in other exhibitions experienced similar problems and have cautioned American artists against participating in the art show.

Page 2

Although I regret that I do not have more specific information to give you, enough evidence is available to reveal a rather shady operation on the part of the sponsors of the Salons. With this information in mind, I would recommend against participating in the Salon Des Nations at this time.

Again, thank you for your interest in this subject. Please contact me if I can be of further assistance.

Sincerely,

Robert Jenkins
Staff Consultant

RJ:ab

I strongly suggest that studying my comprehensive step-by step review of *le Salon des Nations* agreement is worthwhile in understanding the inherent tendency for deception when entering exhibitions where any doubt exists. Study and evaluate any agreement between you and a sponsoring organization. Is the proposal reasonable and equitable? How or why were you singled out for invitation? Will participation reap real benefits and enhance your prestige in the art community or will it leave you embittered toward a method of creative exposure which should have been a worthwhile and fulfilling experience?

The *Salon des Nations* is merely one of many "invitations" from overseas. As long as inexperienced and susceptible artists demand quick recognition without investigating the consequences, such organizations will continue to flourish.

Outdoor

The outdoor show is the most available exhibiting opportunity. These productions attract more viewers and buyers in a single day than a major indoor show does in weeks. The sense of timidity that seems to prevail when attending a museum exhibition vanishes under outdoor conditions. The public enjoys the freedom of informality, wandering in spacious surroundings, and communicating with participating artists.

Outdoor shows have a mixture of fine arts and crafts. Requirements vary. You may automatically qualify for some, and face a selection jury in others. These practices are similar to indoor group shows with some beneficial exceptions. For one, you are permitted far more entries. This advantage has given birth to the itinerant artist who travels far and wide in a van loaded with artworks. Many have earned excellent reputations and substantial incomes in outdoor shows.

Space makes this possible. A sponsoring organization provides a set amount of space for which you pay a fee. Within this area, you are to assemble your own display unit. Some artists construct their own. Others purchase metal units sold by several manufacturers. (Check for free brochures in your art magazine advertisements.)

In essence, you are having a one-person show. When a piece is sold, it is removed and replaced by another. If you feel strongly about its potential as a prize winner, do not remove it until the jury has completed its review and has presented the awards.

Some organizations assemble long, winding snow fences in various open facilities like parks, town squares, playgrounds, and even city streets, and measure off numbered spaces for participants. Twelve feet of fencing provide you with twenty-four feet of hanging space using a variety of methods. Basically all you need are several S hooks and your prewired paintings. Most artists assemble simple bins for unframed works.

Sculptors and craftspeople provide their own tables or stands and use the ground to display larger pieces. If you design jewelry or other small items, hinged display cases are advisable. Some crafts are totally restricted. The prospectus is usually quite clear in listing unqualified entries. Things sometimes forbidden include crocheting, knitting, millinery, velvet painting, horticultural displays, kit jewelry, casts from commercial molds, *decoupage,* and picture frames. Many outdoor shows refuse crafts completely. Knowing the limitations is your responsibility.

I must counsel you about so-called original works of art. Copies of old masters, any other artist's works, any magazine or calendar photographs, or any image which is not your own work is cause for disqualification. Using your own photographic efforts as reference material is acceptable. These rules hold true for any competitive exhibition. Additionally, your application and fee to enter constitute a commitment to exhibit. Sales in any show are considered revenue and are subject to all tax laws of the state where you are exhibiting.

The success of outdoor shows can be attributed to many factors: weather conditions, space availability, and quality of work. If you live in the South, Southwest or on the West Coast, opportunities are limitless. The outdoor show surpasses any indoor activity during the exhibition season. Florida is among the most active areas, drawing artists from thousands of miles away.

In colder Northern regions, outdoor seasons are shorter but no less active. Some may be as modest as small-town, local, and unrestricted one-day shows, with others much larger and lasting for a week or more. The Greenwich Village show in New York City may be considered the grandfather of outdoor shows. It's world renowned and seen by thousands of people.

Many organizations judge not necessarily by media category or individual creative works but by your overall quality. In such cases juries are "charged" not to award a single work which may be superior to the others but to the artist who is consistently proficient in his or her total display. One piece may be chosen for the awards ceremony as representative of the group.

Restricted

Until recently there were few restricted exhibitions, but like doctors and lawyers, artists have become specialists, banding together in particular disciplines. Each group aims to advance its medium. Methods, materials and new developments are topics of discussion during their gatherings. Prospective members are reviewed and elected to membership. These specialists do not confine themselves to restrictive shows but run the full gamut of group activity. Some artists working in various mediums join several special groups and enjoy the benefits of each.

Following are examples of restrictions besides those dealing with media requirements.

The Douglaston, New York, National Art League sponsors an annual national competition for all artists sixty years old or over, with most mediums accepted. *Oi Japan-America Sumi-E* Club sponsors an international exhibition open only to *Sumi-E* artists. The Tri-County Easter Seal Society in Harrisburg, Pennsylvania, assembles a show restricted to physically disabled artists. A Virginia group confines its participants to those residing within a seventy-mile radius of Fredericksburg. The National Society of Painters in Casein and Acrylic limits mediums explicit in its name. The American Watercolor Society accepts only water soluble mediums in a rather broad spectrum, including transparent, acrylic, gouache, and others.

In Atlanta, Georgia, the Southeastern Wildlife Art Show restricts entries to those implied by its title. In New York, the American Artists Professional League accepts only realistic works. In Camden, South Carolina, the American Academy of Equine Art sponsors a show restricted to horse subjects.

You will find shows restricted to women only, to Italian-Americans, to veterans, to Polish-Americans, and to black artists. Fraternal, religious, and ethnic art groups form to maintain a personal identity as well as a common purpose.

Commercial/Industrial Competitions

At one time a "competition" was intended to define an entirely restricted and limited opportunity. But in recent years, some have come to resemble open art competitions. Competition sponsors (as opposed to art organizations, art centers, museums, and the like) were once business and industrial organizations as well as trust fund groups. The first two types of sponsors sought to solicit participants to interpret a product or image. Many still do. For example, some years ago, a major distillery sponsored a competition to depict a single product for use in its advertising campaign. Artists were permitted to use any medium, mode of expression, and discipline, provided the product was recognizable as such in the artistic interpretation. No entry fee was charged, and rules and regulations were binding. In this approach the major difference was (by comparison to the broader definition of art competitions) that the artist had no freedom of choice in subject matter.

These efforts not only handsomely rewarded the winning participants, but there was the residual publicity which contributed to the sponsor's cultural image.

Trust groups administer funds provided by art benefactors which offer opportunities to creative people. Money is awarded as scholarships to classes of recipients designated by the benefactor. Younger artists are the primary beneficiaries.

Although the frequency of such competitions is diminishing, some are still actively pursuing their purposes. The Courage Center of Golden Valley, Minnesota, which sponsors the Courage Card Annual Art Competition, welcomes disabled artists to submit Christmas and note-card designs for reproduction to benefit the Center. Those of you physically unable to pursue a more active art schedule may find this type of opportunity more acceptable.

One organization confines its participants to graduating students at accredited art colleges in the United States. Awards include complete pages in its *RSVP* publication, plus cash prizes.

Another organization sponsors an all erotica competition offering only purchase prizes.

Hallmark Cards holds a National Jigsaw Puzzle Design Contest open to artists and photographers. The exhibition is held in conjunction with its jigsaw puzzle championships.

Residuals

There are two types of residual benefits—those initiated by you and those you achieve through accomplishment and reputation. Self-initiated residuals depend on your ability to capitalize on an exploitable situation. Other residuals come in many forms such as a media source interested in doing an interview with you. Residual benefits represent the area most neglected by artists at every level.

There are several sources available for you to use to gain recognition for your accomplishments. One is a publicity release.

Take advantage of your exhibition success. If you won

an award in another state, capitalize on your success by publicizing the event locally. Submit a publicity release to your local newspaper describing the exhibition and honor received. Newspapers welcome releases. Some newspapers are committed to the arts and devote complete sections to art activities.

With your release, submit an 8x10 black-and-white glossy of your award-winning work. If you don't have a print, get one from the sponsoring organization. You may also wish to send a glossy black-and-white portrait. Clearly identify each picture on the back. The award print should include your name, title of the work and its size, medium, sponsoring organization, and the prize you received. Use a thin, soft magic marker. Pressure applied by a ball-point pen will emboss the image side of the print.

Donating a piece of art to a school, library, hospital, the Boy Scouts, Girl Scouts, museum, town hall, or any of the fraternal organizations has its own rewards. It shows a willingness to participate in the cultural enrichment of the community.

Biographical publications are another potential source for exposure. These volumes print profiles of people and their achievements, artists included. Some limit their entries to artists. Inclusion is based solely on past performance. These publications are widely distributed and are indispensable reference sources. If the purchase price is a prerequisite for inclusion, ignore the offer!

As your reputation grows, you may receive invitations to participate as a judge in an art show. Never refuse a judging assignment based on a fee level. Consider the fee an honorarium, and accept graciously. Some organizations select member judges and pay no fee at all. These artists serve their group. Other art associations develop fee schedules based on the prestige and reputation of those invited to judge.

Demonstrating is another way of exposing your creative techniques. This residual benefit requires self-confidence. Success depends largely on a willingness to face occasional problems. Repeated demonstrations will build your confidence. Many artists have cleverly and expertly worked their way out of tight corners with audience good humor and respect. To teach simply by speaking is one thing, but to speak and create simultaneously is a real challenge.

Questions

Following are some questions often asked.

Q. *Is it possible to earn a living from exhibiting?*

A. Yes, under certain conditions. My feeling is that exhibiting competitively, although potentially remunerative, provides rewards that are more substantial than money. Statistics show that one of every four artists holds more than one job. This allows an artist sufficient income for materials to create artworks. Furthermore, 40 percent of the average income of an artist is earned by artistic efforts. That income amounted to $6,400 in 1981.

Q. *Do I need formal art training to succeed?*

A. Not necessarily. Countless successful artists have either been self-taught or informally trained. A degree in fine arts or certification from a qualified school is no guarantee of success.

Q. *Do politics exist in art organizations?*

A. Neither I nor anyone else is privy to such information. But in my opinion, very little, if any, exist. To be accused of practicing politics could be an unerasable slur on one's character.

Q. *Is there favoritism in competitive exhibiting?*

A. Art teacher judges sometimes have been accused of favoritism by accepting their students' work in order to encourage them. I don't know of any teacher who ever did this. If such questionable conduct is practiced, it is an exception.

Q. *Is it necessary to have a studio?*

A. Not at all. Perfect facilities do not an artist make! I know a successful artist who paints on a kitchen table.

Q. *How much should I charge for my work?*

A. Prices are based on many factors, the most important being an artist's reputation. Renowned artists always command high prices. You may gain more by pricing low and disposing of early efforts, thereby spreading your art around. Prohibitive pricing may leave you with a roomful of stacked works. The effort, cost, medium used, and time expended are also considerations.

Q. *How do I know if my work is any good?*

A. A judgment made at an early stage in your development is not a valid one. Give yourself time to grow. Make comparisons between your early and later efforts, and you will answer your own question.

Q. *I like to draw and paint. Should I become an artist?*

A. No! An artist rarely asks. Either you are or you aren't. Many have buried their desires for years, but a true artist's need to create eventually surfaces.

Q. *How can I become a member of a national organization?*

A. Write to the organization for information. Requirements sometimes appear in the prospectus but most often in the exhibition catalog.

Chapter 2

PROSPECTUS WHAT IS IT?

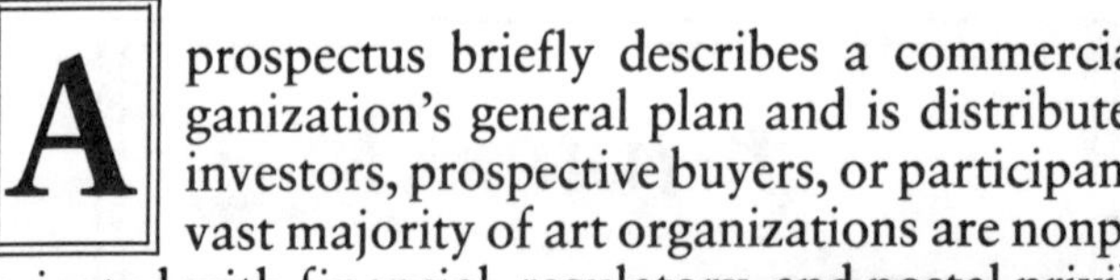

A prospectus briefly describes a commercial organization's general plan and is distributed to investors, prospective buyers, or participants. A vast majority of art organizations are nonprofit oriented with financial, regulatory, and postal privileges. Its officers, directors, and committee members are unsalaried volunteers dedicated only to the organization's cultural advancement. There lies the major difference between the two: a commercial enterprise seeks profits and an art organization does not.

Aside from the semantics, let's get to the heart of the matter. We will examine thoroughly the prospectus and its language. Read each prospectus carefully to establish your requirements. Do not assume too much or you may wonder how, where, and why you erred. A thorough understanding of the regulations will help you avoid potential pitfalls.

On the local level, a prospectus may be a simple announcement with minimal requirements stated. State, regional, and national exhibitions usually include more detailed information based on slide submissions, shipping, and several other factors. International shows are complicated and should provide U.S. customs procedures. Outdoor shows are not unique except for regionals and nationals, which impose sets of requirements specific to their own structure. A prospectus is not just an invitation to participate. It is also an agreement between you and the sponsoring organization, often requiring your signature in acceptance of specific terms. Should you breach any of the conditions, you may be denied the opportunity to participate or be automatically rejected. None of this will happen if you comply with the requirements.

A new requirement has been included in the prospectus regarding some outdoor shows. An artist is not allowed to put a surrogate in charge of his work. The requirement states that the "artists must be present" during show hours.

Regarding indoor exhibitions, some prospectuses state that removing a work is forbidden. Sponsoring organizations will not tolerate empty spaces in a display.

Another breach is failure to deliver or ship your accepted work. If your piece is stolen, lost, or damaged, write or call the sponsor to explain the circumstances. Based on the organization's policy, you may be asked to ship another comparable work which would be reviewed by the board and accepted based on their approval. Or, they may request that you submit another slide of equal quality.

Without adherence to these basic rules, our whole competitive system would collapse. Remember, good habits are synonymous with artistic maturity.

By the same token, you, as a participant, have certain rights and options. Do not submit your work if you feel that conditions and restrictions described in the prospectus seem unfair or unreasonable. However, you may limit your participation in some very worthwhile exhibitions.

Express your views and offer constructive suggestions regarding your concerns. It may take time to see any results since a committee in charge of revising the contents of the prospectus would have to convene, evaluate the proposed changes, and present its findings to the board of directors. Even if a favorable decision is reached, it could take a year or two to revise and print the new prospectus. Unless your voice and those of other artists are heard, the organization must assume that what it is doing in its prospectus is acceptable.

Furthermore, you have a right to express your displeasure over conditions which put your displayed work in jeopardy. Do not show indignation or remove your work. Request that your work be hung elsewhere and explain why. If your request for reasonable consideration is denied, then whatever action you decide to take is understandable. Removal of your work is one action and a written complaint to the board of directors of the organization is another.

The Prospectus

Each requirement shall be specified by a heading, examined and compared to other prospectuses. I will confine these to a representative group of organizations, citing similarities and differences and combined with factual case histories where appropriate. Standard features include the following:

1. Name of Organization
2. Exhibition Dates
3. Juror and/or Juries
4. Judging by Slides
5. Eligibility and Limitations
6. Delivery and Return of Works
7. Entry Fee/Insurance/Liability
8. Awards and Sales
9. Members/Associate Members/ Nonmembers

Combined with these sections are various cautions and organizational unconformities or inconsistencies. Watch for seemingly simple pronouncements that require sharp wits and a keen focus.

1. Name of Organization

An organization's name may be misleading. It's only when you become involved with an organization that its operations are clarified. For instance, the Butler Institute of American Art in Youngstown, Ohio, has its own exhibition facility. Many art associations do not. They depend on the generosity of culturally oriented institutions. The San Diego Watercolor Society holds its annual exhibition at the Grossmont College Art Gallery. Until recently, the American Watercolor Society was considered a permanent tenant of the National Academy of Design in New York. Gallery space was rented for the duration of a show. This privilege was denied to several other national organizations when the Academy's policy was revised, forbidding the use of its facility to outsiders. These groups were forced to find other quarters to continue their annuals. Some applications are made to museums, libraries, colleges, commercial galleries, and other facilities for hanging space. Arrangements may be temporary or for indefinite periods. Groups with greater prestige are given priority and often alternate between two or more quarters on a biennial basis. This is particularly true of state shows, requiring you to deliver your works to a different location every other year.

Consequently, contact with organizational personnel is usually not made in person. It is made primarily by mail, since officers and directors conduct business from their homes, at meetings, or at annual exhibitions. Membership in a group will provide you with valuable information and news that would otherwise be hard to find.

In January 1983, New York Artists Equity Association Inc., through its Network Committee, proposed a plan to the leading area art organizations to participate in buying or renting permanent exhibition space. Seventeen art groups and The Fine Arts Federation of New York (a nonexhibiting organization) supported the proposal.

Each of these organizations sent a delegate to represent them at the committee meeting. Fund-raising letters were sent to their membership, requesting a one-time, tax-deductible contribution of $25, refundable by June 1986 if exhibiting space was not found by that time.

With active support from the 4,000 members of the seventeen art organizations, Artists Equity hoped the plan could be in effect by the fall of 1985. As a functioning entity over a period of time, The Visual Arts Center (as it will be named), having raised the "seed money," would be able to apply for grants from the New York State Council on the Arts and from the National Endowment for the Arts. Additionally, the Visual Arts Center would solicit support funding from the corporate sector and private foundations.

How will the Visual Arts Center function? A board of

directors, composed of artists and business professionals with an understanding of the visual arts and with expertise in fund-raising, will guide the center. A paid professional director will work with each group to handle sales, the daily business of the center, and assist individual organizations (acting autonomously) in preparing their own shows, installations, and advertising. Each organization will carry not only its own name but the Visual Arts Center logo as well.

2. Exhibition Dates

Dates of various exhibitions should be entered on your calendar to maintain a working schedule. Under Record Keeping, I will describe and illustrate methods of accurately logging every piece of work submitted.

3. Jurors and/or Juries

Most organizations list their jurors. In rare exceptions you may read: "Jurors to be announced at a later date." Whatever the policy, a profile of a juror or jury is sometimes included, listing past and present positions in the art community and noteworthy accomplishments. The policies of each organization are as diverse as their methods of judging and selecting awards. The San Diego Watercolor Society uses two jurors to review slides and one for awards. Jurors for the Hudson River Museum Annual in Yonkers, New York, give on-site awards during the opening reception. This unusual method adds excitement and drama to the occasion, motivating all participants to attend. The American Watercolor Society employs seven jurors for selection and three for awards. Noteworthy for efficiency and fairness are two national organizations: Allied Artists of America, Inc, and Audubon Artists, Inc. Each uses separate juries of selection and awards in each media category. All Allied jurors are elected members who volunteer their services. Audubon uses a member jury of selection and a non-member jury of awards. Butler Institute forms a committee, names not mentioned, to select from slides, and one juror for awards. The Cooperstown Art Association employs a three-person jury of selection in the fine arts category, which includes paintings, graphics, drawings, and mixed media. A lone juror serves in the sculpture category and all awards are selected by one juror. For crafts (ceramics, glass, metal arts, and textiles) a juror is used for both selections and awards. Cooperstown's effective method is based on past experience with the total number of entries in the various media categories.

4. Judging by Slides

With few exceptions, the slide submission method is universal. In arranging an exhibition schedule, evaluate your options and make reasonable decisions based on one of the following possibilities:

1. A slide submission and work shipment if accepted. A rejection, although unfortunate, minimizes your expenses as opposed to—
2. Shipping a work and absorbing charges both ways when rejected if the slide submission method is not used.

Slide requirements are somewhat standardized now with few exceptions, namely—"35mm, 2″ × 2″, in cardboard mounts only." Some organizations accept plastic mounts, but unless the prospectus is specific, do not use them. Glass and metal mounts are not acceptable. Identifying a slide is also fairly standard and clearly stated: " . . . place all requested information on the face side." This is particularly critical when a mirror image of numbers, letters, and words is to be avoided.

Butler Institute of American Art states, " . . . The committee will exercise the privilege of rejecting any painting that does not fulfill accurately the image shown on the slide."

The Hudson River Museum's 69th Annual requests two slides, " . . . one should be an overall view and the other a detail. Those who believe that the detail will not aid the jury in understanding their work need not submit the second slide." Hudson River further states, " . . . three-dimensional work should also be represented by two 35mm slides. One of the views should show an indication of scale. Extraneous objects should not be photographed with the sculpture to show scale."

Black and white prints are preferable to slides in the North American Sculpture Exhibition in Golden, Colorado. North American explains: "Each artist may submit up to three black and white views of each sculpture entered, plus color prints if deemed necessary."

A new policy is being adopted by many organizations regarding non-conformity of either slides or photographs to the works they represent. Judgment is based on comparison and, as stated by The Pastel Society of America, leaves at least some leeway: "Accepted art works received which differ *significantly* from the slides will be excluded." This explains, in part, why slides or prints are retained by the organization until the exhibition is assembled. On the other hand, rejected slides or prints are automatically returned with your notification card.

5. Eligibility and Limitations

This section emphasizes eligible media and who may enter. The prospectus usually states its position clearly. Check requirements carefully, particularly age limitations.

For example, Southeastern Watercolorists II at the DeLand Museum in Florida states: "Open to all artists, 18 years or older . . . ," and names the states included. Alexander Lee Nyerges, Executive Director of the DeLand Museum, explains: "The main reason we limit the Southeastern Watercolorists' competition to artists over 18 years of age is to keep the caliber of education and experience high." This policy is reasonable and is not intended to discriminate against any age level. A line must be drawn somewhere and over eighteen seems a universally accepted maturity level. Unless otherwise stated, all ages are eligible.

Every organization imposes limitations in one form or another. Without restraints the system of open exhibitions would be uncontrollable. You are bound by these limitations by agreement.

Southeastern Watercolorists II imposes (lenient) size limitations by stating: "Works must not exceed 80″ in any dimension, including frame. All work must be framed, have hanging wire, and be suitably prepared for public viewing."

By comparison, Audubon Artists, Inc. limits oils to 50″ in any direction including frame, aquamedia to 44″; graphics to 40″, either framed or unframed and covered completely in plastic; sculpture in the round to 24″ x 34″ x 80″, reliefs to 30″ in either dimension and both limited to 300 pounds. Acrylics not under glass will be judged with oils. Sculptors must account for placing their pieces, and those from adjoining states must supply their own pedestals. It further states: " . . . original work in all media never previously shown in an Audubon Annual. Entrants may submit in only *one* category."

Again, referring to the North American Sculpture Society prospectus: "This exhibition is limited to hard sculpture in a permanent medium. Work must be original, and no class-instructed work is eligible. All work must be priced and for sale." In essence, North American forbids work constructed of soft or pliable material, e.g., apple-faced figures, inflatables, or the like. "Work must be original," does not prevent you from submitting a bronze casting, and "class instructed work" is a phrase that tests your maturity as an artist. Also, you may not put N.F.S. (not for sale) on your piece, so resist sending a sculpture that you intend as a gift to your favorite Aunt Millie one day.

The Hudson River Museum Annual states: " . . . fine art in all media, except film and video, which has been completed since 1980 will be accepted. Open to all painters, graphic artists, sculptors, and photographers." Strict requirements apply to prints: "Photographic prints, excluding colored ones, must have been printed by the entrant or under his/her supervision."

Organizations apply restrictions based on experiences with media proven to be troublesome: few submissions, insufficient space, difficulty in handling, weight problems, or for any number of reasons. Sculptors and photographers are faced with the fewest opportunities. Craftspeople, also limited, find ample opportunities in outdoor shows.

In the Boston Printmakers' Annual we find something quite different. "No crated entries or framed pictures will be accepted . . . Prints will be exhibited under glass." You may submit only matted works, cut to the nearest inch and covered with a clear plastic material. They impose no size limitation.

The Pastel Society of America forbids copies from other artists or photographs. It judges both members' and non-members' works. The prospectus concludes: "Please do not call PSA as jury results will not be given on the phone."

The Butler Institute requests the removal of screw eyes and wires. Some say just the opposite.

6. Delivery and Return of Works

Failure to record every delivery and return requirement could be costly and chaotic. A calendar, with large squares to note your entries, is a good idea. Mark delivery, rejection pickup, and return, including hours where necessary. Reception dates are optional.

An effective prospectus lists every important date from slide submission to when the exhibition closes under a "Calendar" heading. You may wish to use this for reference purposes.

For example, Butler Institute of American Art is specific and clear with its information and shows unusual leniency in stating: "Deadline for receipt of painting . . . If work is not received by this date, it will not be listed in the catalogue." Some organizations are not so lenient.

By comparison, the San Diego Watercolor Society states: "Selected paintings must arrive by the scheduled date. Those which do not will not be included in the catalogue or considered to be part of the exhibition."

Butler Institute emphasizes that delivery by shipment must be made, "shipping charges prepaid," and returned, collect, via the same carrier unless notified otherwise. It adds in bold capital letters that artists who send work "PARCEL POST ARE REQUIRED TO MAIL A LIKE AMOUNT OF THE CHARGE." Shipping will be examined closely under Framing and Shipping. Butler cautions: "Regarding hand deliveries, work must be picked up no later than _____ or will be subject to disposal."

In my inquiry to Louis A. Zona, Director of the Butler Institute of American Art, I requested an explanation of the term "disposal." He responded immediately and clarified the prospectus statement:

"If a work in a juried exhibition is not picked up by the specified date a phone call is made directly to the artist. An alternate date is then set for pick-up, and if that is not met, another call is made before disposition of the work.

"We are a small institution with extremely limited storage space. If we do not adhere to such a policy, storage would be at a crisis level and could endanger all stored works of art."

The North American Sculpture Exhibition clearly states: "Shipping instructions will be mailed with notification of acceptance." Several groups employ this method.

The American Watercolor Society makes two distinctions in its delivery requirements:

1. It accepts only uncrated deliveries from those able to deliver by hand.
2. Shipments must arrive at a carrier agent one

week before receiving day to allow for uncrating and delivery.

Consider what was said under *Name of Organization* in the beginning of this section. Many organizations, AWS being one, do not have their own quarters. On receiving day hand- and agent-delivered works will be assembled and organized by a committee especially chosen for the task. I can assure you that a delivery at any other date, whether by hand, mail, or whatever, will not be received by anyone.

Regarding return of exhibits, AWS continues: "All works must be removed by the artist or his accredited agent . . . " An agent in this instance means anyone authorized to pick up your work. "All work not so removed will be stored at the artist's risk and expense."

Hudson River Museum is, by far, the most strict. "A storage fee of $3.00 per day will be charged for work not picked up on stipulated dates. No exceptions will be made. Unless special arrangements have been made with the Museum's registrar, works not claimed by __________" (30 days from closing date) "will become Museum property and will be sold at public auction."

7. Entry Fee/Insurance/Liability

These sections, although part of every prospectus, will be examined under a separate chapter.

8. Awards and Sales

Awards, both in number and monetary value, vary significantly from one organization to another. The amount of sales commission charged also varies. With some exceptions, prestige of an exhibition is usually synonymous with the higher monetary value of the prizes it offers. And bigger and better awards do not require higher entry fees. The reverse is often the case. The only problem you will encounter is stiffer competition. But you should "gamble" anyway in spite of the competition; if not to win an award, at least to gain acceptance.

Butler Institute offers cash awards and makes available up to $10,000 for purchases to be added to their permanent collection.

The North American Sculpture Exhibition offers a total of $6,000 in awards. In contrast to Butler's 10% sales commission, North American takes 30% of the artist's selling price as stated on the entry form.

Allied Artists of America, Inc., itemizes every medal and cash award, averaging $12,000 in watermedia, oil painting, and sculpture. Allied makes every effort to promote sales, requesting a 20% contribution on all transactions. They will consider N.F.S. (not for sale) on your label but P.O.R. (price on request) is forbidden. The restriction on P.O.R. is understandable since Allied cannot negotiate by phone with you and a prospective buyer. Handled another way, American Watercolor Society accepts P.O.R. on its labels but considers the work N.F.S.

Southeastern Watercolorists II offered cash and purchase awards totalling over $2,000 in its 1984 show which was given at the discretion of the juror and the DeLand Museum.

Boston Printmakers' commission is 33 1/3 percent and it holds that the "artist must assume expense and responsibility of supplying to purchasers any additional prints which may be sold at exhibitions" (annual or traveling).

9. Members/Associate Members/Non-Members/Membership

You will not find this subject covered in all prospectuses, because some, such as art centers, museums, and colleges, are not membership organizations. Nonmember sponsors solicit entries for open annuals from the general population. Member groups solicit their own and other interested artists.

There are other differences. Member organizations allow members to enter without paying a fee. Annual membership dues cover fees. Also, acceptance in an exhibition is often automatic. These privileges result from stringent membership qualifications.

Membership in these organizations is available to you if you apply and meet their requirements.

Audubon Artists, Inc. requests a fee, slide, entry and jury cards, and a stamped, self-addressed envelope from nonmembers. Associate members in good standing pay no fee, submit a slide, entry and jury card, and an SASE. A full member in good standing submits an entry card only.

Membership in Allied Artists of America, Inc. is by invitation only and follows the same procedure as Audubon except to alternate jury exemption on an odd and even year basis. Members are jury-exempt in odd years only. Each year an *ad hoc* committee selects a limited number of candidates from participants in the annual exhibition and proposes them to the board of directors for a final decision. Sustaining associate members are actively involved in the life of the organization, may hold the office of treasurer or assistant treasurer, and participate in the board's activities. Associates enjoy all the privileges of membership, are listed in the exhibition catalogue, are invited to opening receptions, annual meetings, and may submit news items to and receive copies of the A.A.A. Newsletter.

The American Watercolor Society applies similar rules with one significant difference. All entries, from members, associate members, and nonmembers, must pass a jury of selection and awards. Consideration for membership requires acceptance in three AWS shows during a ten-year span.

Butler Institute, a nonmember organization, makes no distinctions for entry. It's open to anyone wishing to submit.

The Kentucky Watercolor Society passes all entries before its juries and awards *automatic* membership to any artist whose works have been accepted into three aqueous shows. Simply complete a membership card and submit your dues. Your qualification will be checked according to records.

Cautions

It is interesting to note that some cautions which benefit the organization also benefit the artist. For example:

1. The Audubon organization states "only first class mail will be accepted."

2. Mainsail Art Festival, sponsored by the city of St. Petersburg, states:

The violation of any Festival rule " . . . may result in the artist being asked to remove his exhibit and/or in the artist's ineligibility for future Festivals.

"All applicants must include a business size envelope with sufficient postage along with application, fee, and slides. The committee will not be responsible for responding in any manner to any applicant who fails to provide this return envelope."

3. One organization's prospectus requires an award recipient or a representative to be present at the reception or face forfeiture.

4. Another group "charges" its juror with the right to transpose, divide, or combine categories when necessary.

5. Allied Artists states in bold capital letters: "NO WORK LISTED IN THE CATALOG MAY BE REMOVED BEFORE THE CLOSING OF THE EXHIBITION."

6. The North American Sculpture Exhibition rules as follows: "Submission of an entry obligates the artist to have the work available if accepted."

7. Hudson River says: "We reserve the right to reject any entry not meeting the specifications in this prospectus and not suitable for museum display."

By now you are fully aware of the finality of prospectus content. Once more lenient in their attitude, organizations are stiffening and enforcing prospectus requirements.

Some measures may seem unjustly severe but you must appreciate that most problems are self-imposed. Each new warning found in a prospectus is not arbitrarily made but based on, and compounded by the artist. With this understanding, your participation concludes a mutually agreed-upon covenant that asks nothing more than the cooperation of all concerned.

The American Watercolor Society, like many others, states in bold letters: "THIS PROSPECTUS CONTAINS ALL THE NECESSARY INFORMATION. PLEASE READ IT CAREFULLY AND KEEP IT FOR REFERENCE." If, indeed, any question needs to be asked, my experiences have shown that organizations will comply to a reasonable written request for the answer.

The following list includes a cross section of art organizations. You may be early or late for current shows, so ask to be placed on the mailing list.

Pastel Society of America
The National Arts Club
15 Gramercy Park South
New York, NY 10003

The Hudson River Museum
Hudson River Annual
Trevor Park-On-Hudson
511 Warburton Avenue
Yonkers, NY 10701

Audubon Artists, Inc.
Annual Exhibition
225 West 34th St., Room 1510
New York, NY 10001

The Allied Artists of America, Inc.
The National Arts Club
15 Gramercy Park South
New York, NY 10003

American Watercolor Society
Annual Exhibition
Salmagundi Club
47 Fifth Avenue
New York, NY 10003

Boston Printmakers
National Exhibition
299 High Rock Street
Needham, MA 02192

Cooperstown Art Association
Annual Art Exhibition
22 Main Street
Cooperstown, NY 13326

The Butler Institute of American Art
Annual National Midyear Show
524 Wick Avenue
Youngstown, OH 44502

Kentucky Watercolor Society
P.O. Box 7125
Louisville, KY 40207-0125

The North American Sculpture Exhibition
The Foothills Art Center
809 Fifteenth Street
Golden, CO 80401

Western Colorado Center for the Arts
Annual National Art Exhibit
1803 North Seventh Street
Grand Junction, CO 81501

Edson Art Center
Iron Horse Festival Art Show
418 Front Street
Logansport, IN 46947

Wind River Valley Artist's Guild
National Art Exhibit
Box 26
DuBois, WY 82513

National Watercolor Society
Dorothy Sklar, Exhibition Chairman
6612 Colgate Avenue
Los Angeles, CA 90048

Mainsail Arts Festival
P.O. Box 2842
St. Petersburg, FL 33731

The DeLand Museum
Southeastern Watercolorists
449 East New York Avenue
DeLand, FL 32724

Questions

Q. What can I do if I don't understand a prospectus requirement?

A. If time allows, write or call the organization for an answer. If you do not receive an answer, reconsider submitting your work.

Q. *Is there any difference among the terms "Aquamedia," "Watermedia," "Aquarelle," and "Watercolor?"*

A. None. Each term describes a water soluble medium. Whichever one an organization uses is merely a matter of preference. Aquamedia and watermedia are not standard dictionary words, whereas *aquarelle* is French and derived from the Italian *acquerella,* water color. (*Aqua* is Latin for water.)

Q. *I was an hour late in my hand delivery and was refused entry. Is that fair?*

A. Were *you* being fair?

Q. *Will my fee be refunded if I cannot honor my commitment?*

A. You have one of two choices:

1. Forfeit your fee.
2. Write or call to explain the problem. I cannot give you a precise answer since the decision will be based on organizational policy.

Q. *Why do some organizations list their awards and others do not?*

A. Policies dictate whether a group lists awards or not. Some organizations have a predetermined amount to offer and are therefore able to divide their awards according to media. Others may specify an approximate amount. Many simply announce a total amount. These terms allow an organization necessary leeway for last minute donations as well as possible cancellations. (Awards money is obtained primarily from entry fees and by public and private support.)

Q. *Am I entitled to attend the opening reception even if I was not accepted?*

A. An opening reception or preview is open to the public unless stated otherwise in the prospectus. Some organizations have private previews open to show participants and invited guests. Others combine the event with cocktails and/or dinner and charge a fee. Whatever the case, I strongly suggest attending those available to you. Knowing your competition is a vital part of the system. It heightens your awareness of techniques and brings you in contact with others in the field.

Q. *I notice that some organizations are particularly tough in their membership qualifications. Why is that?*

A. Organizations set standards to maintain a level of quality. Specialty groups employ criteria which often seem insurmountable. I suggest joining groups using limited requirements as a first step.

Chapter 3

MEDIA

My intention is not to discuss media, *per se*, but how the media relate to the exhibition process.

Historically, the traditional media continue to be included in all exhibitions, while others suffer from a constant ebb and flow of organizational interest. This flux promotes fewer opportunities for some, while others are literally barraged, forcing them to make wise exhibiting decisions.

Your interests should not be influenced by the wider acceptance of one medium over another. However, it is in your best interests to explore all the media before making choices. And don't hesitate to break out into new areas: e.g., drawing begets print making and vice versa; pure watercolor begets acrylic, the latter eligible as both aqueous and oil mediums. Diversify wherever the transition is possible.

Originally, I had three interests—oil painting, watercolor, and detailed pencil renderings. Initially, I devoted my energies to oils with occasional excursions into watercolor and pencil. An exquisite group of watercolors at an aquamedia exhibition reversed my interest from oil to watercolor and pencil. Field trips to augment a watercolor repertoire of reference material generated another propensity for both pen and ink and marker sketches. These experiences support my contention that:

1. Multimedia creativity is more rewarding.

2. Whether involuntarily or by design, many artists explore several media to maintain greater interest in the creative process.

3. The availability of opportunities is in direct proportion to the extent of your involvement.

To better understand and evaluate media involvement, let's examine the system from these levels:

1. A review of media;

2. How they influence organizational preferences and why.

Recent innovations in media have perpetuated exhibition problems for both artist and organization. Statistically, the participant faces conditions requiring greater understanding of historical data. We will review the various media, make comparisons, and briefly describe each one's place in the current selection and award process. To avoid unnecessary lateral digression, all water-based media will be placed under one category called aquamedia. The following are those categories most frequently included in the prospectus:

1. Oil painting
2. Aquamedia
3. Drawing
4. Sculpture
5. Pastel
6. Mixed media
7. Prints
8. Photography

Oil Painting

Statistically, oil painting is at the top of the list over all other media. Priceless masterpieces in oil predominate on the walls of museums everywhere. It's only in modern times that we have witnessed the inclusion of other two-dimensional media. Oil painting is still the medium practiced by a majority of artists. However, art organizations exercise no control over media and have introduced categories and awards based on the following:

A numerical imbalance of oil paintings versus other media warrants an equal imbalance of selection and awards.

A distribution of awards based on this imbalance.

Aquamedia

Not until the early nineteenth century did aquamedia receive any measure of acceptance. The English acknowledged exercises in watercolor as a prerequisite of refinement, and in natural settings, landscape painting in watercolor became popular.

It wasn't until the twentieth century that watercolor attracted a school of serious exponents: Charles Burchfield, with his fantasy-oriented quality; John Marin, with his vibrant and energetic expression; and Winslow Homer, who earlier brought prints of his wind-swept illustrations to the attention of Americans across the country. From these modest beginnings, aquamedia can now boast a large following of practitioners in traditional and innovative blends of pigment. As long as water remains the catalyst, there is no dividing line in describing watercolors. Acrylic, the most versatile of these media, is acceptable either as an aquamedium or oil, depending on its presentation.

The American Watercolor Society states under "Works Eligible": ". . . aquamedia on paper, unvarnished. Absolutely no collage and no pastels . . ." Conversely, The National Watercolor Society includes a broader range of eligibility, stating in part: "Pastels and collage, if used, must be in conjunction with watermedia. The final decision in all cases rests with the jury."

Unless the prospectus says, "includes all aqueous media," check the ones listed to determine your eligibility.

Drawing

This category includes pencil, ink, drypoint, charcoal, and others. As expansive as aquamedia, it suffers from limitations and is excluded from some exhibitions. It is not denied because of artistic significance, but rather on statistical grounds, proving that competitive interest is lacking. Unless an organization receives sufficient entries to warrant its inclusion, it removes the category from its prospectus. On the other hand, unless drawing exponents find sufficient opportunities, they simply do not submit. Based on this unfortunate paradox, drawings are often categorized with other media.

Sculpture

The history of sculpture can be traced to 20,000 years ago and found in many ancient cultures, among them the Egyptian, Babylonian, Roman, Greek, and others. Sculpture constituted one of the major disciplines in man's earliest involvement with the arts.

The interest in sculpture waned but resurfaced during the Renaissance; a period most historians agree flourished in Europe somewhere between the fourteenth and sixteenth centuries.

Sculpture often achieved the same distinction that was given to the painting masterpieces that came out of this age.

After another waning period, sculpture has reemerged in the past few hundred years. It enjoys considerable status today. But the medium faces obstacles in our current system of open exhibitions. It causes space, security, and display problems by inhibiting traffic flow, and posing a potential for damage as a freestanding object.

The sculptor, in turn, is faced with personal problems. If his interest is "bigger," he may be forced to seek opportunities outside the competitive system, since eligibility is restricted regarding size and weight by organizations and shipping carriers. Limitations apply to all media, but sculpture is the most vulnerable.

More and more prospectuses state, "media, all except sculpture." Remember that inclusion of a medium category in a prospectus is the only basis for eligibility unless the statement reads, "all media."

Serious efforts are being made to accommodate the sculptor as groups mount exhibitions aimed in their direction. The Radford Foundation of Radford University, Virginia, sponsored a show in 1984 open to any ceramist and sculptor. The Salmagundi Club in New York sponsors a show of photographs and sculpture only. The Foothills Art Center in Golden, Colorado sponsored "The North American Sculpture Exhibition" eligible to artists in the United States, Mexico, and Canada. Under "Work Eligible," the following, somewhat confusing, statement appears: *"The assembling at Foothills of any accepted work is the responsibility of the artist."* My inquiry to Regina Hogan, Director of Exhibits and Events, provided the following answer.

"The phrase 'The assembling at Foothills of any accepted work is the responsibility of the artists' refers to any sculpture that involves complicated and laborious procedures in order to construct the finished product. It also pertains to the popular 'assemblage' sculptures that are spontaneous creations and require the talent of the artist to complete the work of art."

Pastel

This medium, often combined with others under a single category, suffers the same fate as drawings. Sponsoring groups pay limited tribute to this form because of entry imbalances. Nevertheless, pastel artists are forming societies in increasing numbers to exploit their works and promote its acceptance. One organization clearly implies that works must be predominantly pastel to be accepted.

Mixed Media

This term, found in many prospectuses to categorize a group of media, is actually a misnomer. In an effort to include a battery of media under one classification, organizations simply list them as mixed media. A collage is one interpretation of mixed media but so are combinations of watercolor and pastel; watercolor, ink, and pastel; watercolor, ink, and pastel, and any other conceivable mixture. It is your responsibility to ascertain in which category your work belongs.

Prints

The art of printmaking is a relatively recent development. Perhaps the earliest printed objects found in Europe were playing cards printed in Spain in the fourteenth century. Almost concurrently, Johann Gutenberg of Germany invented the movable type printing press. From these modest beginnings, engravings, etchings, lithography, serigraphy (silkscreen), and many other processes made both single and multicolor repeat images possible. The extent to which print techniques have diversified has caused organizational problems. Some organizations exclude them altogether, while others depend on the "lumping system." These practices have again given rise to the inevitable—the printmaker's show.

Photography

In spite of this medium's acceptance as an art form, many still consider photography unrelated to the "fine arts." Both still photography and cinematography have been described as mixtures of art and science.

The significance of photography is evidenced by the 18,000 prints recently purchased by J. Paul Getty for the Los Angeles Getty Museum, valued at $20 million. The Metropolitan Museum of Art in New York City has 10,000 photographs, some extremely rare.

Organizational policies regarding photography are as broad as those affecting drawings, sculpture, pastels, mixed media, and prints. Apart from out-and-out exclusion, some restrictions are reasonable, as can be seen in the Hudson River Annual prospectus under—"Eligibility": *"Photographic prints, excluding colored ones, must have been printed by the entrant or under his/her supervision."* As with any print media, Hudson River is asking that the artist is in control of, and responsible for, the total concept.

Media Influence—Numbers and Awards

In itemizing media we have only touched upon their importance and acceptability. It is significant to note that only limited numbers of organizations, mostly those with national scope, list media categories and the extent to which each is honored.

The following statistics are drawn from Allied Artists' seventieth annual exhibition of December 1983-January 1984. All percentages are in round numbers.

a. Oil Painting

Of 106 accepted oils, 18 percent received $4,950 in awards, amounting to 35 percent of the total $14,050.

b. Watercolor (includes pastel)

Of 94 accepted watercolors, 18 percent received $5,400 in awards, amounting to 39 percent of the total $14,050.

c. Sculpture

Of 69 accepted sculptures, 16 percent received $3,700 in awards, amounting to 26 percent of the total $14,050.

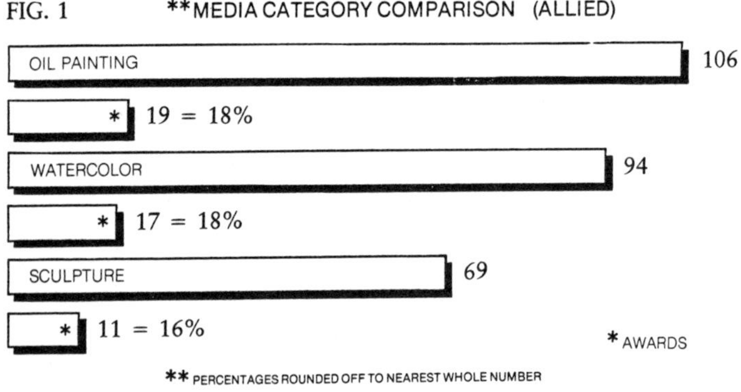

Figures 1 and 1a clearly illustrate the relationship in a, b, and c.

Of significance is the difference between the watercolor and oil dollar amount distribution when compared to award percentages. Few organizations strike such a balance. Equally as important, Allied's prospectus lists every award by category.

FIG. 1a *DOLLAR AMOUNT DISTRIBUTION (ALLIED)

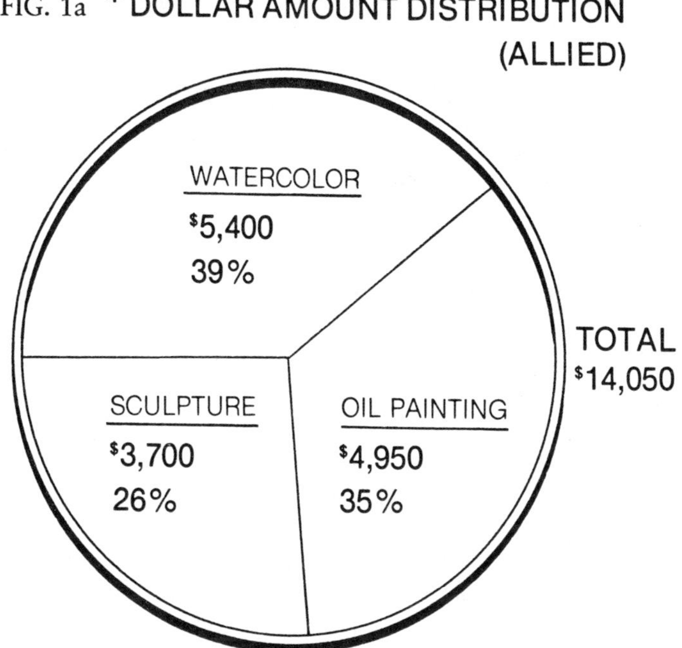

* PERCENTAGES ROUNDED OFF TO NEAREST WHOLE NUMBER

Audubon Artists, Inc. (no connection with the Audubon Bird Society) is just as fair in its distribution of awards and dollar amounts. Percentages are minimally out of balance, whereas the dollar amount seems to favor oils. The latter is based on circumstances beyond Audubon's control. Some data will help.

As explained in "Prospectus—What Is It?," many organizations are faced with limited exhibition facilities that force drastic revisions in scheduling. Having lost its tenancy rights at the National Academy of Design in New York City, Audubon found new quarters at the National Arts Club in New York. Insufficient space prompted Audubon to hold its exhibition in two parts. Part One included *aquarelle*, sculpture, and graphics to-

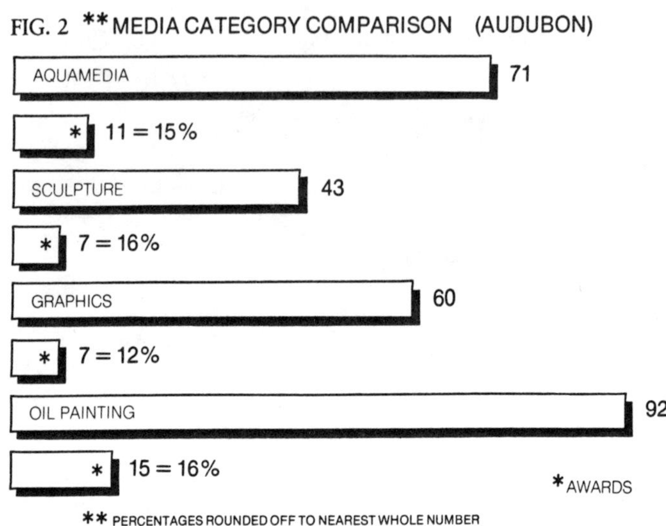

taling 174 works, while Part Two consisted of 92 oils. This dichotomy, although related under one banner, presented enough distinction to avoid media competition between the two parts.

Second, percentages of awards in Part One compare favorably with Part Two. (See Fig. 2 and Fig. 2a.)

The difference in dollar amounts favoring oils over *aquarelle*, sculpture, and graphics combined (Fig. 2a) is not as extreme as it appears. Almost half of the oils' dollar amount is based on memorial award funds. That means:

1. A member of an organization establishes a bequest in his will, to a medium of his choice, in a specific dollar amount, period of time to remain in force, and how distributed.

2. Donations are solicited to establish an award fund in honor of a departed member or philanthropic patron.

3. Anyone may contribute a specific amount of money or merchandise in his or someone else's name. The award may be made once, or as often as the donor wishes.

4. Or, you may designate an award to honor someone dead or alive.

Allied Artists, Audubon Artists, and other national organizations form fund-raising committees, strive for equitable distribution of awards dollars, and itemize all awards in every media category as a matter of policy. They elect a vice-president and three directors for each media category. The American Watercolor Society and The Pastel Society of America, specializing in one medium, also list every award. This policy is not common on all levels.

FIG. 2a * DOLLAR AMOUNT DISTRIBUTION (AUDUBON)

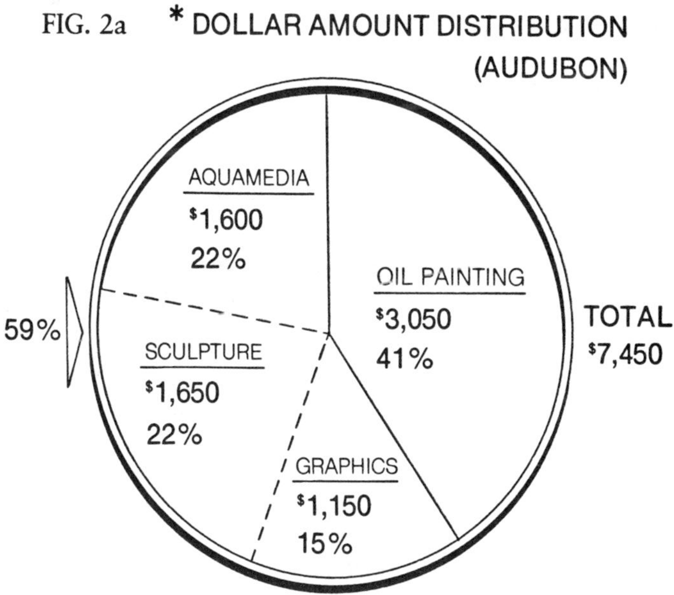

* PERCENTAGES ROUNDED OFF TO NEAREST WHOLE NUMBER

The majority of organizations do none of these things to allow for flexibility in both dollar amounts and numbers of awards. Clues can be found in every prospectus. The San Diego Watercolor Society and Southeastern Watercolorists II give cash and purchase awards totaling over $8,000 and $2,000 respectively.

The Hudson River Museum and Butler Institute do not list awards by category or dollar amount breakdown. The Iron Horse Festival lists media, painting, drawing, sculpture, ceramics, textiles, metals, woods, and glass (photographs excluded), awarding a total of $1,750. Distribution of these funds is typical of the tendency to give the highest award to "Best of Show" and equal first, second, and third prizes in "Paintings," and a category combining all other media. This is not meant to show preferential treatment but is due to the age-old problem of media entries imbalance. Finding more equitable methods is a difficult task for those without committees to study and evaluate the situation.

Questions

Q. *Why are such great restrictions put on size?*

A. Three factors control this limitation. (1) Availability of wall space. Some groups prefer not to crowd display walls by controlling media eligibility. (2) Mobility and ease of handling is a concern when hundreds of works are involved. (3) Available manpower to receive, uncrate, hang, remove, recrate, and return entries.

Q. *Is my technique of adding watercolor washes to an ink drawing considered an aquamedium or a drawing?*

A. It can be either. Unless stated clearly in a prospectus, a sponsoring group that accepts both media will decide where it belongs. Under some conditions, where purity of medium is defined, i.e., "all transparent watercolors only," your work would not be eligible.

Q. *My medium is oil, and I prefer working in large sizes. Does that create a problem? What are my options?*

A. Yes, it does create a problem, and your options are limited. Keep alert for those rare opportunities when media size is not a factor. Also, consider supplementing your normal output with others eligible under prospectus guidelines.

Q. *Can I enter more than one medium in a show?*

A. Yes and no. Check the prospectus. Some allow it, and others clearly state, "Each artist may enter one work only, regardless of category."Another may say, ". . . up to three slides of paintings only, from which no more than one is to be chosen."

Q. *I purchase ceramic castings which I paint in great detail. Is this considered original work and eligible for entry?*

A. No. It would fail every test in both sculpture and craft shows where judging is a prerequisite for acceptance. Unless the creative effort is 100 percent yours, you will be limited to shows with similar entries.

Chapter 4

SUBMISSION SLIDES AND PRINTS

A camera is an important piece of equipment for your particular purpose and should include certain features. A "Single Lens Reflex" (SLR) 35mm camera with a 50mm lens is basic, and with limited accessories, your task is simplified. Any additional equipment is best left to your financial resources, personal whims, and the advice of a qualified camera center sales representative.

Basic Items

1. Single Lens Reflex Camera (SLR)
2. Tripod
3. Cable Release
4. Polarizing Filter
5. Close-up Lenses
6. Easel

These items will range between $275 and $400, depending on the features. The differences will not affect slide quality proportionally but will provide additional versatility. Since these basic items are made to last for years, this initial investment is not prohibitive.

My SLR, priced at $149.95, has proven easy to manipulate while producing excellent results. My cable release and tripod, purchased over twenty years ago, show little sign of wear. Similar items now available have not been improved upon to any great extent. A polarizing filter is essential under certain conditions. A hand-held exposure meter is standard equipment for the professional, but you may forgo this expense and rely on the one built into the camera. Close-up lenses are required primarily for miniatures. The magnifier, although optional, is a device worthy of your consideration.

As a last resort, you might research used equipment. A reputable camera center will explain reliability, life span, and warranty limitations of resales. Check the classified ads of your newspaper for flea markets and garage sales for items which can be tested on the spot—such as tripods, cable releases, and easels.

Camera—35mm Single Lens Reflex

The SLR is the most important weapon in your arsenal, despite the cost, because the reflex system allows you to see what the camera sees. Non-SLR's contain restricted exposure areas potentially detrimental to subjects where perimeters are critical. Additionally, SLR cameras are easy to use, lightweight, available in both manual and automatic modes, and constructed of durable materials. A manual mode camera is less expensive but still very effective. All major companies manufacture manual mode cameras in which both aperture and shutter speed are set manually. The LED (Light Emitting Diode) display tells you what shutter speed the camera recommends. This allows exposure adjustments while looking through the viewfinder. Quartz-timed manual mode cameras provide more accurate shutter timing, resulting in better exposures.

Some centers will accept your old camera as a trade-in for replacement parts or will service it for resale. Unless you need the cost savings, I suggest keeping your old camera for other purposes. A reflex camera loaded with slide film and the other with print film provide instant photo opportunities on both fronts. Prints, whether they be landscapes, cityscapes, seascapes, human figures, interiors, or still lifes, are an invaluable source of reference for potential subject matter.

For instance, some artists pressed for time use an opaque projector (one that projects a reflective image—a photo print, for example) to "size" a subject image for transfer onto paper or canvas. A drawing or roughly painted interpretation is superimposed directly over the projected image and this eliminates hours of preparation. Slide projectors serve the same purpose and are widely used among commercial illustrators. Norman Rockwell shot dozens of photographs of posed individuals and groups as reference material for his paintings.

Renting is another possibility. Ritz Camera features a rental service with 160 nationwide locations. You could rent an SLR for a weekend. Cameras range from $4.00 to $7.50 per day and $7.50 to $18.00 per week. This alternative may help determine your preferences, the camera's efficiency, processing results, and minimize your investment until a final choice is made. With a rental, be prepared to shoot a sufficient number of works to justify the expense. It is also possible to work out an agreement whereby your rental fee is deducted from the cost if you decide to buy.

Tripod

Ansel Adams, the renowned nature photographer, who published his first book in 1930, lugged a tripod across America's vast western terrain to guarantee the quality he demanded. The tripod not only supports and steadies your camera but leaves you free to perform other functions. Even the most inexpensive tripod would be better than none. It establishes a constant focusing distance from camera to subject, which is of particular importance when your works are identical in size. As sizes vary, you can move either the tripod or subject backward or forward.

Although you can spend as little as $12.95, I suggest you investigate tripods in the $40.00-$60.00 price range. The tripod features listed below will simplify the shooting process:

1. Three section braced legs
2. Three way panhead
3. Geared elevator
4. Adjustable, nonskid feet

Cable Release

This piece of equipment is as essential as the tripod. It acts as an extension of the camera and is built to operate much like an elongated hypodermic needle. When it activates the camera shutter release, it acts as an "antishakes" remedy. No professional photographer would consider shooting fixed objects (copying) without a cable release.

Polarizing Filter

This filter is attached to the front of the lens and when rotated helps to reduce reflections. It has little value with drawings and other dull-finished mediums but proves quite successful when photographing glossy oil paintings and any subjects under glass. I would recommend a polarizer when you need a slide for a work that you prefer not to unframe. A polarizer has a gray tint in the glass which will not adversely affect color fidelity.

Close-up Lenses

Close-up lenses on SLR cameras reduce the focusing distance from nine to six inches or less. My set contains three rings and proper focusing is achieved by testing one, a combination of two, or all three. Their use still permits you to shoot exactly what is seen through the viewfinder. Aside from miniatures, they are useful in isolating small sections of larger works to study and evaluate details of painted passages, pastel density, ink or pencil strokes, or any number of creative techniques.

Easel (Floor or Table Top)

This device is a worthwhile investment not only for supporting works when shooting slides but as a display for studying completed pieces. An art supply catalog will simplify your selection with an assortment of shapes, sizes, construction materials, and prices.

Inexpensive, aluminum, triangular tabletop easels to support small canvases, watercolors, and other two-dimensional subjects may be adequate. From this basic style, easels can be over nine feet high with casters, ratchets for height adjustment, and made of solid oak.

I would suggest investing in an easel suitable for multi-use purposes, preferably one with height adjustable supports. I use a tubular aluminum floor easel to support my works. It's portable, lightweight, and sturdy, and sells for around $40. This easel features telescoping, skid-proof legs with folding spikes for outdoor use, adjustable height supports, and an overhead clamp to provide backward and forward mobility from a vertical position.

Optional Items

1. Light exposure meter
2. Magnifier
3. Floodlights

The first two are not absolutely necessary, but they add a measure of sophistication to otherwise basically adequate equipment. The third item may be useful under certain uncontrollable conditions described in the slide-shooting process.

Light Exposure Meter

Although many artists, myself included, have managed slide control without a light meter quite successfully, a representative of Ritz Camera Centers suggests that using one provides an extra measure of exposure accuracy in certain conditions. Sculpture, for instance, with its myriad configurations and variety of materials, produces highlights and shadows which may require separate readings, their values recorded, and averaged. With this information, your camera adjustments can be determined easily enough.

Framed subjects with strong light and dark values can also be checked and averaged. An 18 percent gray card is normally used in these circumstances. However, your SLR camera with its built-in meter is also effective in evaluating reflected light. Furthermore, by employing a method called "bracketing" (more on this later) results similar to a light meter's potential are possible.

Magnifier

You may wish to consider a magnifier for your copy work, particularly in combination with close-up lenses.

This useful focusing tool doubles the image size to reduce any margin of error when rotating the lens focusing ring. Whether your camera has a horizontal or diagonal split image, or microprism in the center of its focusing screen, the magnifier reduces the problem for those with vision impairments. Nearsighted and cataract surgery artists are usually dependent on this visual aid. Remember that what may appear in focus when viewing a slide against daylight or an incandescent bulb may not be when projected and enlarged many times on a viewing screen. Both proper focus and color fidelity play important roles in your chances for acceptance by a jury of selection.

Floodlights

Floodlights offer an optional method of shooting slides for those who live and work in colder climates where long winter months, snow-covered ground, and short natural light periods present limited photographic opportunities. This piece of equipment is composed of a clamp, reflector, and a high wattage bulb.

Film

I've excluded film from the equipment list since it must be replenished and constitutes a continuing cost factor. I recommend Kodak brand film. For our purposes Kodachrome 25 (KM 135-20) and Kodachrome 64 (KR 135-20) will be used exclusively.

Kodachrome 25 is a color slide film with excellent color quality, extremely fine grain, and high sharpness. These characteristics are possible because of its low speed. But it's also recommended for bright light conditions. Nevertheless, ASA 25, combined with the versatility of the SLR manual mode, can be effective under less-than-perfect lighting situations.

Kodachrome 64 has almost the same characteristics as ASA 25 film, is one-and-a-third stops faster, and is also suitable for less than ideal light.

If you are willing to experiment and make comparisons, try Kodak Ektachrome 64 (ER 135-20), a daylight film which gives excellent color rendition, sharpness, and very fine grain structure. Ektachrome 160 (ET 135-36) is a high speed film best suited for outdoor daylight with good grain characteristics and sharpness.

Many of you will require black-and-white 8x10 submission prints. Of Kodak's most used types, the Panatomic-X (FX 135-20 or 36) film is best for enlargements from 35mm size negatives. It combines fine grain black-and-white film with high sharpness when used under good lighting conditions. Plus-X Pan (PX 135-20 or 36) has almost the same qualities as Panatomic-X and performs well in all but the poorest light.

A word of caution about buying film. Check the expiration date on the carton. Be sure the roll has a long life span.

Remember that artworks take a back seat to slides and prints during the early stages of exhibition procedures.

If your photographic attempts are less than successful, my advice is not to submit that slide. It's better to buy more film and try again than to waste the time, energy, and money in submitting less than your best.

Shooting the Subject

Now that you have your photographic equipment, it's time to test your skills. Trial and error, experimentation, failures and successes will increase your knowledge and enhance your confidence. However, with patience and attention to detail, success is possible even with your first shooting session. Let's consider this first effort as a trial run by testing a roll of Kodachrome 25 and 64 slide film or Panatomic-X and Plus-X Pan for black-and-white prints. These trials, if successful, will produce both usable slides and valuable data for future reference. Furthermore, comparisons between the two slide films and black-and-white films will help decide future preferences, *provided your tests are conducted under similar conditions.*

We will follow a step-by-step procedure as listed and then add a final review.

1. Film Loading
2. Tripod (Camera support)
3. Easel (Subject support)
4. Lighting/Viewing/Focusing
5. Aperture and Shutter Control
6. Bracketing
7. Data
8. Multiples
9. Film Unloading
10. Processing
11. Results
12. Artificial Lighting

1. Film Loading

Begin with either Kodachrome ASA 25 or ASA 64 film. Your camera brochure will illustrate proper loading procedures. Check the following to minimize any potential problems:

1. Carefully insert the film leader into the camera's film take-up spool slot.
2. Take slack out of film.
3. Most important: Both upper and lower teeth of the sprocket must be properly engaged in the film perforations to prevent slippage.

Set the film speed, ASA 25 or 64, by rotating the film speed dial until the index shows the correct ASA value on the scale. Insert the film carton end flap into the space provided behind the camera as a future reminder of film brand and number of exposures. This is particularly helpful when the whole roll is not used in one session. The film speed is recorded on the index dial. But will you remember the brand and number of exposures in the roll? I have forgotten a few times, until I learned to save the end flap. If your camera does not have a frame for this purpose, use tape.

2. Tripod (Camera Support)

Connect the camera to the tripod panhead and check for wobbling or slipping. Do not overtighten. Extend the legs until the tripod stands firmly, and then raise the center height adjustment post to one of two positions:

a. High enough to avoid bending and straining your neck and back if you prefer to stand, or

b. Adjust the height so the viewfinder is level with your eye, while you are in a comfortable sitting position. A stool is preferable to a chair to avoid accidental contact with the legs of the tripod which could upset its position, your focus, and the alignment. Initially, you may find this method unwieldy compared to holding a camera in your hand. But in a short time, you will feel more relaxed and comfortable.

Attach the cable release to the shutter release button-socket until the screw sits comfortably. Don't force it. Test the cable action by depressing the plunger (listen for the shutter's clicking sound) and advance the film lever. Repeat until the exposure counter stops at number one.

3. Easel (Subject Support)

Your subject matter is now ready to be prepared for shooting. Two-dimensional works can be supported in one of several ways. How a work is photographed is optional:

1. Prints and Drawings—matted or framed
2. Watercolors, Pastels, and Mixed Media—unmatted, matted, or framed
3. Oils—unframed or framed

For unmatted subjects:

Tack (pushpin) your subject to plywood or other rigid board large enough to accommodate your largest work. Mark all four corners with a felt pen as a future positioning guide for identically sized subjects. Repeat this procedure for any size, remembering to store the board for your next shooting session. These markings are usable for vertical images as well by merely rotating it ninety degrees and positioning the subject in the horizontal guides. (See Fig. 3.)

Position the mounted subject on the easel's adjustable height supports perpendicular to the floor by maneuvering the overhead clamp. Your camera and work are ready for shooting.

FIG. 3 UNMATTED SUBJECT

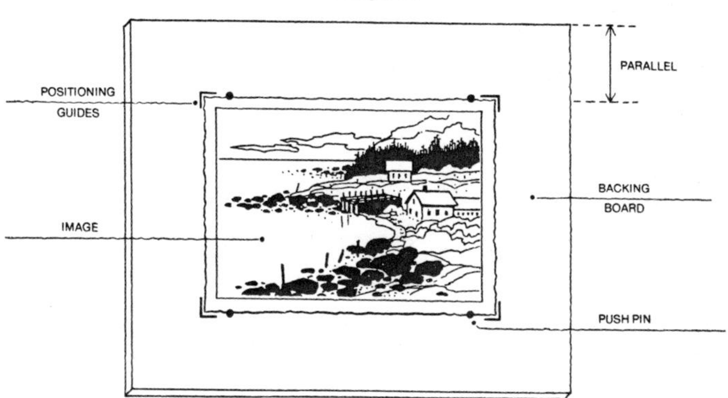

4. Lighting/Viewing/Exposure

Lighting

Where to set up your equipment depends on available light. Conditions need not be ideal considering the versatility and range of the camera's light-emitting diode (LED), to be discussed under "aperture and shutter." Using natural indoor or outdoor light has proved successful in my experiments. Check these conditions.

a. Light sources
b. Time of day
c. Maneuverability of equipment

We've already discussed light sources, and we should understand how the light's origination influences the results

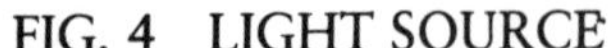

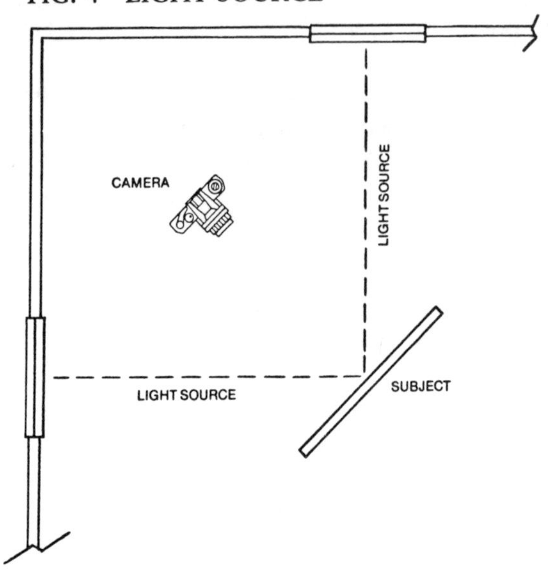

FIG. 4a LIGHT SOURCE

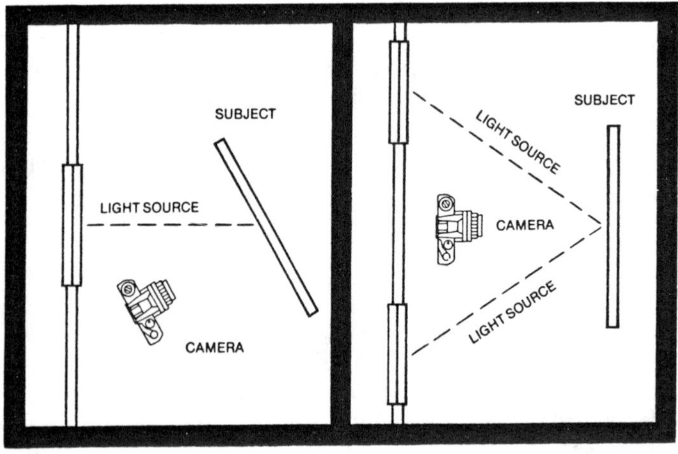

you'll have in shooting your subject.

Condition b., time of day, means shooting your pictures between two hours after sunrise and two hours before sunset.

Condition c., maneuverability, means allowing enough room to set up and shift your tripod and easel to allow you room to maneuver.

Figures 4 and 4a illustrate choices available. I've used all three, providing an adequate range of aperture/shutter speed combinations.

Viewing and Focusing

Position your camera and tripod parallel to the subject by adjusting either your tripod pan or the easel. (See Fig. 5.) Center the lens on the image, and check the corners of the viewfinder to capture as much of the image as possible vertically and horizontally.

FIG. 5 CAMERA AND SUBJECT POSITIONS

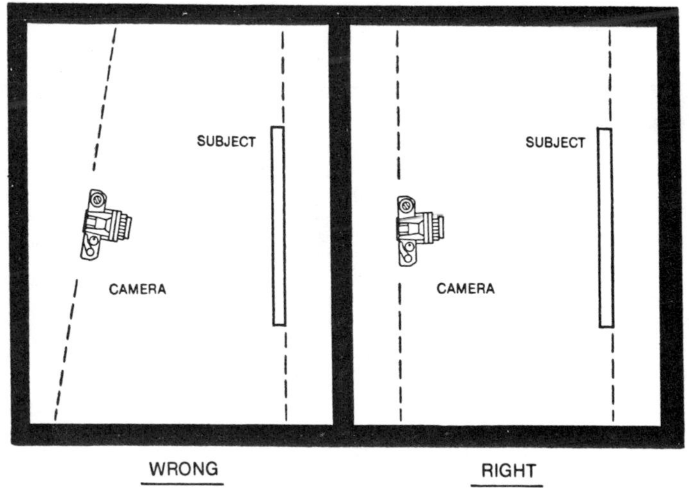

Adjust your equipment until everything is locked into position. Unless it is in direct proportion to the slide size, 24mm x 36mm which convert to .945″ x 1.47″ or approximately 15/16″ x 1 3/8″, capturing the total image isn't possible.

Example: Image size 16″ x 20″

Multiply the decimal equivalent of the slide, .945 x 1.417 by 14. You will get this result:

.945 (24mm slide) x 14 = 13.23″
1.417 (35mm slide) x 14 = 19.838″

The equation shows the smaller dimension to be 2.77″ less than the image size of 16″. The larger dimension is acceptable with a .162 decimal difference. To compensate for the 2.77″ loss, adjust your camera until the viewfinder divides the difference top and bottom, provided there is no significant loss of image. (See Fig. 6 and Fig. 6a.)

FIG. 6 SLIDE AND IMAGE PROPORTIONS

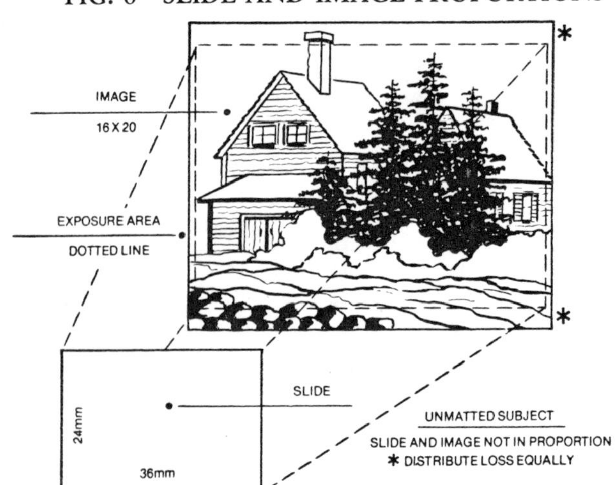

I don't want to bore you with mathematical equations. Rather, my intention is to prevent confusing surprises for you. Nor do I suggest that all subjects can or should be proportionate to the slide. But there will be times when you need or want to take slides of unmatted subjects and do your matting and framing at a later date.

You will now focus on your subject through the SLR optical system. Focus by rotating the focusing ring until a portion of your subject is sharpened by one of several methods, depending on your camera:

Horizontal split image
Vertical split image
Microprism
Combination of microprism and split image

No one focusing system is superior, and none is critical in your camera choice. You will adapt to one which is described and illustrated in the accompanying literature.

FIG. 6a SLIDE AND IMAGE PROPORTIONS

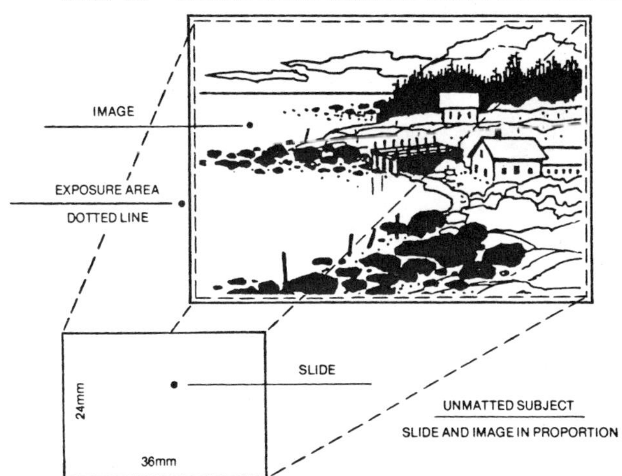

I shall digress temporarily from the discussion of photographic procedures to describe how to prepare matted, framed, and three-dimensional subjects for maximum exposure. Choice of method is a matter of preference.

Matted

Let's presume you wanted to shoot the same 16″ x 20″ subject to avoid image loss. Matting is one way. However, the out-of-proportion condition would still prevail but is now transferred to the mat instead of the subject. Secure your work to a backing board with tacks or pushpins positioned at the outside edge of the mat. When using four-ply mat boards, which should be sufficiently rigid to be self-supporting, use the easel's overhead clamp, and establish a vertical position to the floor. (See Fig. 7.)

FIG. 7 MATTED SUBJECT

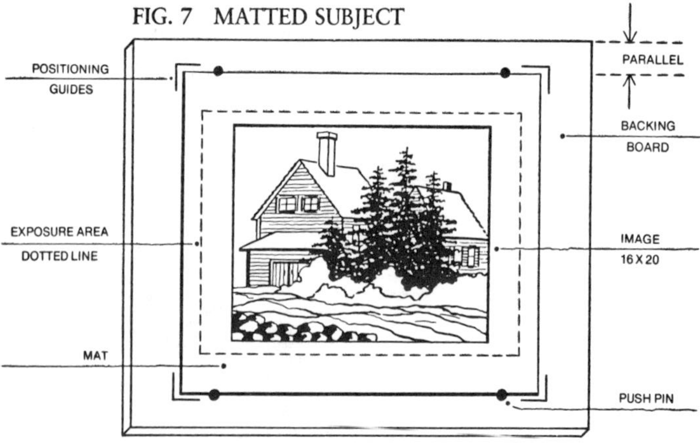

Framed

Oil paintings, aquamedia, prints, pastels, photographs, and so on should be exposed just beyond the limits of the frame. Avoid using the overhead clamp if possible. Instead allow the subject to rest against the easel and adjust the camera to the same angle. An alternate method would be to hang your work on a wall if the light is adequate. For glazed works, it would be wiser to slip your matted subject into a frame without glass: expose, remove, and insert others. If you must shoot through glass or shoot a highly varnished oil painting, use a polarizing filter.

Three-Dimensional Subjects

If your needs are black-and-white prints for three-dimensional or two-dimensional subjects, the process remains essentially the same. Place your subject on a pedestal or tabletop against a solid, neutral background. Sculpture must include its surrounding space. Depending on its configuration, two or more views may be needed.

Now that preparation of subject matter has been reviewed, revolve the focusing ring and concentrate on a portion of the image until a perfect alignment is achieved. Remember, as you focus, the lens moves in or out, changing the viewing distance and affecting the image size slightly. Merely reposition the tripod until the maximum area is covered and refocus. This adjustment is particularly important with unmatted subjects. Matted or framed subjects are not affected. In either case, unless you accidentally jostle the tripod, you will retain proper focus for all same-sized subjects.

5. Aperture and shutter control

Lighting conditions will determine aperture (shutter opening) and shutter speed. These are totally interrelated, one affecting the other, controlled by the aperture ring on the lens called *F stop,* usually ranging from 2 to 16 or higher. Changing an F stop automatically affects the shutter speed, calibrated on a scale anywhere from 15 to 1,000th of a second and higher. The aperture increases or decreases in size, controlled by the F stop ring, and controls the light entering the camera. The shutter opens and shuts at various speeds to control the amount of light acting on the film. This scale varies according to the camera to include slower or faster speeds. Proper exposure is possible in various aperture/shutter speed combinations. Example:

F8 plus 60 (1/60 second)
F2.8 plus 500 (1/500 second)
F11 plus 30 (1/30 second)

All of these will work. As you depress the shutter release button at F2.8, the large opening through which light is emitted needs only 1/500 of a second to expose the subject. At F11, less light is emitted, requiring a longer period of time, or 1/30 of a second.

With all systems "go," you are ready to copy the subject. In my past experiments two methods were used—bracketing and multiples. In bracketing, data recording is a must.

6. Bracketing

Bracketing is one method by which three slightly different exposures are made by varying the aperture control one-half or one complete stop. Set the aperture ring at F8 and check your LED for sufficient light on the shutter speed scale by depressing the shutter release button partway. Move the aperture scale one F stop lower and one higher and check light. If these settings signal "go," then shoot the same subject with each of the three aperture/shutter speed combinations. This is called bracketing. By shifting one stop lower and one higher you are slightly altering the exposure. When compared with your actual subject, the differences you note will determine which slide to use. The following tells you how to record this data accurately for future reference. (See Fig. 8.)

FIG. 8 BRACKETING DATA

EXP.	TITLE	LOCATION	TIME	LIGHT	F STOP	SPEED	RES.
1	SUNSET	INDOORS	12:30 P.M	SUNNY	8	60	
2	"	"	"	"	5.6	125	
3	"	"	"	"	11	30	
4	BARN DOOR	"	1:00 P.M	CLOUDY	4	250	
5	"	"	"	"	2.8	500	
6	"	"	"	"	5.6	125	
7	ANGEL POND	"	1:30 P.M.	"	4	250	
8							

7. Data

When your film is processed, check each slide carefully against your subject and note results in the last column: accurate, overexposed, underexposed. Using A (Accurate), O (Overexposed), and U (Underexposed), mark each slide in pencil near the number of the slide frame. Your A slide will be used for duplicates.

This data recording method may be more costly and time consuming, but it's worth the effort to familiarize yourself with your camera equipment, to understand the nuances—often subtle—of the three exposures, and to guarantee at least one accurate slide for submission and duplication. With this information, you will want to take bolder steps in future shooting sessions. Try this with both ASA 25 and ASA 64 film.

8. Multiples

Multiples is the opposite of bracketing in that you expose one subject two or more times at one shutter/aperture setting. Experience and confidence will lessen the risk, and when your results are a success, provide additional slides for future submissions. I suggest keeping one for duplicates, since you may wish to enter the same subject in various exhibitions over a period of time. There would be no point in reshooting your subject. As with bracketing, keep a data information sheet.

9. Film Unloading

After the last exposure, rewind the film by pressing the rewind button and rotating the crank clockwise until the tension slackens. Pull out the rewind knob to open the camera and remove the film.

10. Processing

Where to process your film requires serious consideration. There are many competent processing labs with proven chemical formulas, sophisticated electronic devices, and knowledgeable people. But their rate of success can never reach 100 percent.

Services range from mail-order facilities to professional labs. Mail-order advertisements are usually found in magazines and Sunday newspaper supplements. This service may be low cost with an average mailing time of one week to ten days but the quality may be inconsistent. and your complaints may go unanswered.

Your local supermarket, drugstore, or camera center also offer processing centers. Here you're relying on a middle-person to forward your film to a photo lab. This method is quicker and slightly more expensive. The results could be the same, or better, or worse.

Professional photo labs can be found in the Yellow Pages of your phone directory, trade publications, or photography magazines. Although their service is the most expensive, quality ranks high, the service is quick—usually within 24 hours—and you will be dealing with labs knowledgeable in every aspect of film processing.

11. Results

Use a projector or natural light to check each bracketed slide against the subject. The acid test is to project the slide at the same size as the subject. Make it even larger, if necessary, to determine any differences in color and sharpness. Pick the best one and save for duplicates. It's important to remember that selection juries will project all slides to one size.

Check your multiples the same way. If successful, all will be of equal quality and usable. Again, save one for duplicates. It's possible that you may enter the same work half a dozen or more times.

12. Artificial Lighting

Floodlight is a common substitute for natural light. Standard equipment is used to "flood" the subject with "light." This is accomplished with tungsten filament bulbs ranging from 125 to 500 watts. The life span of a bulb depends on its wattage—high means less, low means more.

When combined with a dish-shaped reflector, rays are directed toward the work in a wide angle or are narrowly concentrated, depending on the reflector used.

As with most photographic accessories, the life expectancy justifies the expense. For our purposes we will consider the following items:

1. Two blue 250 watt bulbs (BCA Bulb 4800 K, color corrected for normal household lighting with daylight film)
2. Two reflectors
3. Two clamps
4. ASA 64 slide film

Set up your camera, cable release, and tripod. Arrange the floodlights at forty-five degree angles to the camera and ninety degrees to the subject. (See Fig. 9.) Clamp the floods to the backs of chairs. Lightweight, adjustable, and movable stands are also available to support flood units. It's advisable to switch off floodlights while subject matter is being positioned and during long periods of time between exposures.

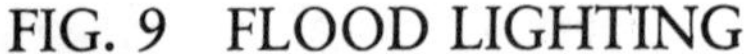
FIG. 9 FLOOD LIGHTING

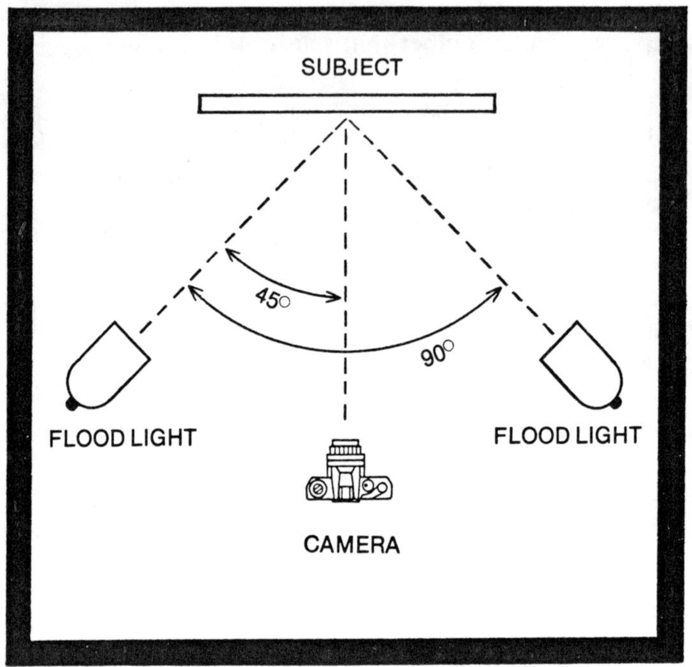

Review
A brief review of the shooting process will highlight significant points.

Film Loading

a. Insert film securely into take-up spool slot.
b. Remove film slack.
c. Engage film in upper and lower sprocket teeth.
d. Set film speed on rotating film dial.
e. Save end flap of film box.

Tripod

a. Connect camera securely to panhead.

b. Connect cable release to shutter release button.
c. Test cable action.

Subject Support (Easel)

a. Extend and firmly lock tripod legs.
b. Adjust movable subject supports to proper height.
c. Position unmatted, matted, or framed subject.
d. Position three-dimensional subject on table or pedestal.
e. Use neutral background.

Lighting/Viewing/Focusing

a. Check light source, indoors and outdoors.
b. Align camera with subject horizontally, vertically, and parallel.
c. Check mathematical equation for maximum exposure of unmatted subjects.
d. Mark backing board at four subject corners for future positioning.
e. Check focus.
f. Check F stop and shutter speed combinations.

Bracketing/Data/Multiples

a. Bracket exposures one stop higher and lower.
b. Check possibility of each combination, using the light emitting diode (LED) in the viewfinder as the primary factor.
c. Accurately record data as illustrated.
d. Determine an effective F stop and shutter speed for multiples.
e. Expose three frames.
f. Record multiples data.

Film Unloading

a. Press rewind button
b. Unfold and rotate rewind knob.

c. Pull rewind knob to release camera back.
d. Remove film.

Processing

a. Mail order.
b. Retail outlet.
c. Processing lab.

Test your options against quality, reliability, and personal contact.

Results

a. Check processing against subject.
b. Project slide if possible.
c. Reserve best exposure for duplicates.

Artificial Lighting

a. Set floods at ninety degrees to the subject.
b. Set the camera at forty-five degrees to the floods.
c. Turn off floods during exposure intervals.

Aside from making slides for submission, photography's application in the creative process is immeasurable when used to record what the naked eye fails to perceive and memory fails to retain. As a source of reference it supplements the sketching tool in building a repertory of visual facts. To learn the potential of the camera there are many books available at bookstores and libraries. Some suggestions:

The 35mm Photographer's Handbook
by Julian Calder and John Garrett
Crown Publishers, Inc., New York

The Single Lens Reflex Handbook
by Michael Langford
Alfred A. Knopf, Publisher, New York

The Photographer's Handbook
by John Hedgecoe
Alfred A. Knopf, Publisher, New York

Questions

Q. Should I make prints of my works?

A. Yes. Have prints made directly from your slides. Keeping an album provides an instant visual review of your works for an interested viewer. Also record in your album the medium, date completed, and title of each subject.

Q. Is it possible to produce a slide to perfectly match the subject in color and detail?

A. A perfect match is not easy to achieve. Also, you can't compare an image reflecting light (subject) with one transmitting light (slide). Even when projected onto a screen, the quality of background differs greatly from the base on which your subject is rendered. At best, you can expect only to *approximate* a match.

Q. What do I do if my annual creative output is limited?

A. Your production can pose problems, but there's a solution: Let's assume your annual output is six submissable works—one piece every two months. Unless you're willing to risk leaving film in the camera for an extended period, I'd recommend a limit of two works per roll which allows three frames for bracketing and three for multiples of each subject, two frames each for detail sections, and the remaining four exposures for reference material. The expense is outweighed by the advantage of available submissable slides.

Q. I paint finely detailed, time-consuming oils in fairly large sizes. My average is two a year. What should I do about slides?

A. Slides are not your real problem; your annual production and sizes are. Regarding size, your exhibition opportunities may be limited. Check the show prospectus to determine your eligibility. Also, producing two works a year further limits your opportunities. Your only choice is to use a complete roll of film for each painting. (This may be a blesssing in disguise by allowing bracketing, multiples, and detailed reference shots for future works.) Inherent in every work is the potential for creating others which is found by close examination of different parts of the work that may be particularly exciting.

Q. *I've checked several cameras and each had different viewfinders. Does this make a great difference in shooting slides?*

A. Not necessarily. Most viewfinders will serve the intended purpose. I prefer one with a vertical, rather than horizontal, split image focus, combined with an LED, and a shutter speed reading scale. This allows manual control of F stops and speeds for exposure flexibility.

Q. *What is meant by film speed?*

A. Each roll of film, whether it's color or black and white, is given a number to indicate its sensitivity to the light reflected from the image. The term "speed" applies to the film's quick reaction to light, much as you would blink when going from a dark to a bright room. Films with high numbers need less light to expose a subject. Conversely, low numbers need more light. Slide film comes in two standard speeds, ASA 25 and ASA 64.

Q. *I'm often tempted to buy sale film from open bins. Why is it so cheap? Is it worth buying?*

A. Its effective life span has passed, as you may note by the expiration date printed on the carton. It may be worth buying, but your chances of shooting successful pictures would be greatly reduced. Film, like many materials that are vulnerable to the ravages of heat, moisture, and age, deteriorates and loses its effectiveness. If you attempt such a purchasing gamble and win, consider yourself lucky.

Chapter 5

RECORDS

To enter a significant piece of information in a log or ledger is less time consuming than tracing the disposition of a completed work.

We will review record keeping under four categories. But first it's necessary to lay out a small investment for items found in an office supplies store to record this data.

Record Keeping Supplies

1. One three ring loose leaf binder with separators (5″x7″ or larger)
2. Ruled binder pages
3. Wall calendar with large date squares
4. 4″ × 6″ index card file box

Record Keeping Systems

1. Production Record
2. Exhibition Reminder
3. Exhibition Log
4. Slide Bank

Production Record

Maintaining a production file is a simple process. Without it, and subsequent related records, your productivity is reduced to guesswork.

The first section of the loose leaf binder will be devoted to listing your works. Divide the page into four columns. From left to right add year, title, medium, and size. (See Fig. 10.) Enter the information immediately after the work is completed. At the end of each year, total the production of each media and media total. Start a new page for each year.

Exhibition Reminder

In our prospectus review I stressed the importance of remembering slide submission, delivery, and pick-up dates. Failure to deliver when your work is accepted is a breach

FIG. 10 PRODUCTION RECORD

1984	TITLE	MEDIUM	SIZE
1/22	VIEW OF THE POND	ACRYLIC	11 X 14
2/10	MORNING MIST	"	18 X 24
2/27	BARN	PEN AND INK	8 X 10
3/9	SUNRISE	WATERCOLOR	18 X 24
3/21	ROCK FORMATION	GRAPHITE	8 X 10
4/3	LATE SNOW	WATERCOLOR	18 X 24
4/29	THE GATE	ACRYLIC	11 X 14
5/12	CLOUD BANKS	WATERCOLOR	18 X 24
6/1	THE BRIDE	PEN AND INK	8 X 10
6/28	VIEW FROM ERLAND'S FARM	W. C. SKETCH	11 X 14

of a contractual agreement. Forgetting a pick-up date may result in serious consequences as decided by an organizational policy.

Hang a wall calendar in a conspicuous area and refer to its notations periodically. When your prospectus arrives check for four possible entry conditions:

1. Hand delivery only
2. Slide submission with hand delivery
3. Slide submission with shipment
4. Slide submission, hand delivery, *or* shipment

Mark your calendar to coincide with one of the four conditions:

1. Notice hand delivery and pick-up dates for rejected and accepted works.
2. Note slide submission date; turn your calendar to the previous month and pick a date as a memory jogger. If and when your slide is accepted, note hand delivery and pick-up dates.
3. Same as number 2 but note shipping date instead of hand delivery date. Include return shipping date to determine work availability for future entry.

4. Same as number 2 but note either hand delivery or shipping date, whichever applies, and return shipping date.

Fig. 11 and Fig. 11a illustrate a calendar reminder for a fictitious exhibition called "Mediafest" which combines conditions numbers 1 through 4.

Although the purpose of a reminder calendar is apparent, it also provides immediate warning to prevent entry overlapping. To prevent this possibility, check all your prospectuses before making notations on your calendar.

It is your responsibility to search out calendar reminder dates. Not all prospectuses simplify the process. Some scatter this information under separate headings, while others confine them to one area.

San Diego Watercolor Society lists not only important data but also reception dates plus gallery hours and other events.

The Pastel Society of America covers all dates in its calendar except for slides submission, which is reported elsewhere.

The North American Sculpture Exhibition covers all dates except for return shipment information, which is reported elsewhere.

Southeastern Watercolorists II mails shipping instructions only to accepted artists. This method is gaining favor among organizations and obviates the need to record unnecessary information on your reminder calendar.

The exhibition log stores information for reference purposes, allows statistical comparisons, and prevents duplication of entry. For example, the system—

1. Records every competitive art exhibition ever entered;
2. Includes the medium and title of every work submitted;
3. Records the size of the work;
4. Shows whether accepted or rejected;
5. Records awards received, if any.

FIG. 11 EXHIBITION CALENDAR

JANUARY

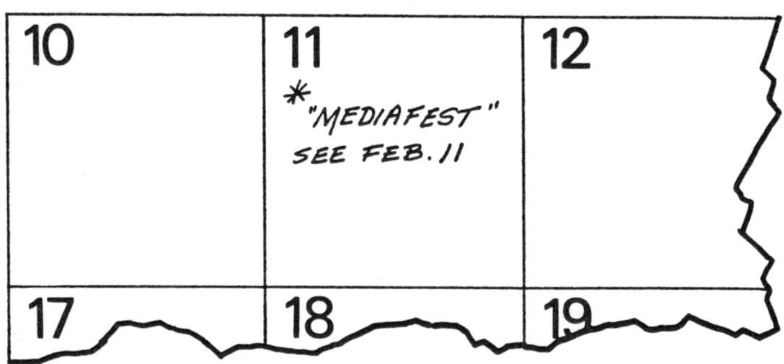

FEBRUARY

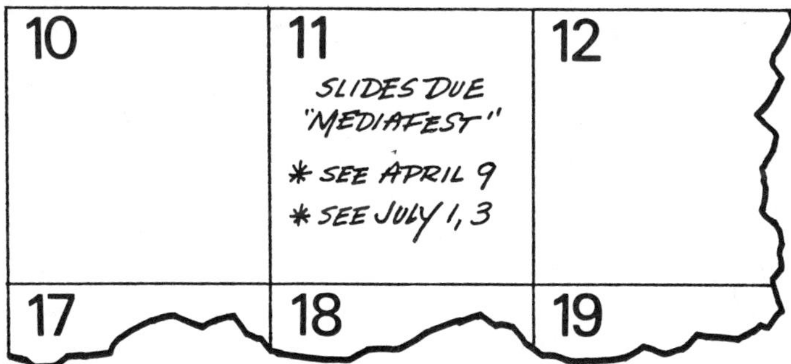

APRIL

9
HAND DELIVERY
OR
SHIPPED WORKS
DUE
"MEDIAFEST"
* SEE MAY 8

10

11

16

17

18

FIG. 11a EXHIBITION CALENDAR (cont.)

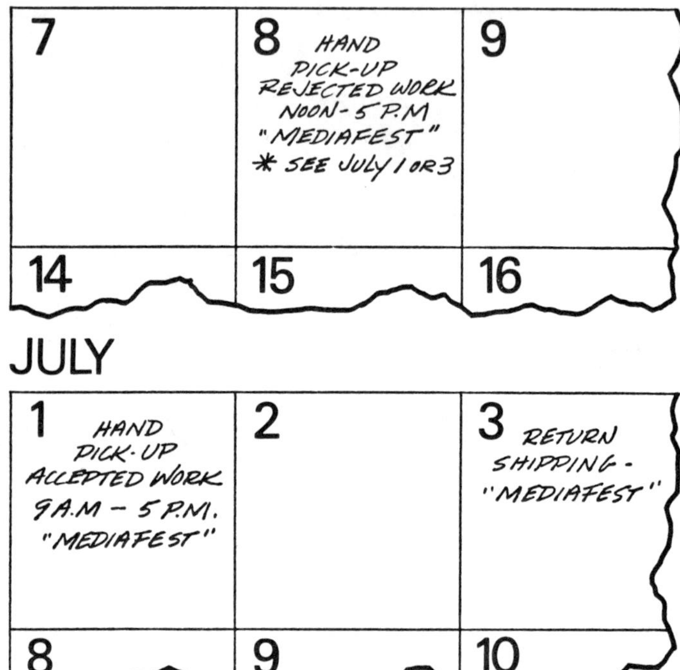

Proceed as follows. (See Fig. 12.) In the second section of your loose leaf binder put the current year at the top of the page. Draw lines as illustrated.

In the first column record the month you hand delivered a work or submitted a slide. This notation helps determine an active or inactive schedule. It may help you decide to increase or decrease your involvement.

In the second column include the organization's name and title, if any, *e.g.* Kentucky Watercolor Society "Aqueous '84."

In the third column record the title or titles of the works submitted.

In the fourth column record the medium (particularly important if you work in several media).

In the fifth column enter the matted or framed size or sizes of the works submitted.

In the sixth column record the jury decision. This entry may come months later but immediate action will prevent its omission.

The seventh column is identical to the sixth, except that it records rejections. The eighth column is similar to numbers six and seven in that an award notification may arrive months after submitting your work.

FIG. 12 EXHIBITION LOG

1984								
	MONTH	ORGANIZATION	TITLE	MEDIUM	SIZE	A	R	AWARD
	MAY	ALLIED ARTISTS OF AMERICA	PECAN TREE	W.C.	28X36	✓		L. GRASS-$100
	JUNE	KENTUCKY W.C. SOCIETY	EARLY AUTUMN SUNRISE	W.C.	24X30	✓		
				W.C.	18X24		✓	
	JUNE	ROCKFORD INTER-NATIONAL	STONES II	GRAPHITE	11X14	✓		HON. MENTION
TOTALS			12			7	5	3

This data is indispensable for reviewing annual successes and failures but more importantly it's a gauge of your career's direction. However, do not use statistical comparisons based on only two years of exhibiting. As you enter higher competitive levels, your log may show a change as these new challenges alter your success ratio.

These ups and downs are normal as you reach higher and higher. Challenges indicate greater risk taken against stiffer competition and it's these risks that test your creativity. Work quality, space restrictions, jury selection based on numbers, all combine to produce circumstances with which your work must contend.

The log tests your approach to selectivity. A lower percentage of successes, either acceptances or rewards, in an annual schedule of prestigious commitments may be limited but may also be truly more rewarding than greater successes in minor endeavors.

Slide Bank

Over the years you may accumulate hundreds of subject slides. Inasmuch as many of these will be submitted several times, an access system is essential since finding what you need should not be left either to guesswork, or to checking each and every container. Whether you own a projector with a square, rectangular, or circular storage tray, or whether your slides remain in their original container, indexing is a simple matter. In each case, subject slides should be kept separate from any others.

Cartons

Slide cartons are adequate in protecting your slides and they stack well. Mark each one with a bold letter, starting with "A" to "Z." Continue with "AA" to "ZZ" if necessary. These letters should be visible immediately when viewing the stack. On 4″x6″ index cards, include a letter corresponding with the carton, subject titles contained, how many of each, and approximate date. The letter "D" in the system is reserved for slides best suited for duplication.

When a submitted slide is returned file it accordingly. Mark each slide with a letter to correspond with the carton, facilitating its storage.

Storage Trays

Slide projector storage trays make indexing even easier by virtue of a standard system of consecutive numbers adjacent to each slide slot. Use the same method as described under "Cartons" but remember to separate slides for duplication.

Questions

Q. *Most art groups forbid the entry of a work twice in the same annual exhibition. Can I submit a work again if it was rejected the first time?*

A. In general terms the answer is yes. The restriction usually applies to resubmitting an *accepted* work a second time.

Q. *Should an exhibition schedule follow a calendar year or what is known as the exhibition season?*

A. With the increase in activity a season is difficult to define. Scheduling by the calendar year makes more sense.

Q. *My work production is limited. How can I get maximum exposure in as many exhibitions as possible?*

A. Keep an accurate record of *submission* and *return of work* dates as found in the prospectus. With this information you can plan a schedule that minimizes overlapping. Since many art organizations tie up a work for months, you might consider submitting to exhibitions that do not.

Q. *How do I avoid getting bogged down with overlapping exhibitions that make scheduling a continuous process?*

A. One way is to limit your exhibitions. Another is to send for your prospectuses early in order to establish a schedule based on exhibition preferences. Keep an accurate calendar reminder and exhibition log that quickly pinpoints your commitments.

Q. *Would you record every preliminary sketch used in the completion of a work or just the actual work?*

A. The choice is a personal one. As I see it, some preliminary sketches are considered to be creative works in many instances.

Q. *Why should I record the completion date of a work?*

A. For several reasons. For one, only in this way can you establish your creative development over many years of productivity. Second, many sponsoring organizations place restrictions on the age of your entry. Your records will provide this data.

Chapter 6

FRAMING
PACKING
SHIPPING

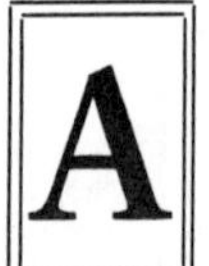n important aspect to consider in framing involves protecting your work from potential damage. Members of receiving committees stack paintings against walls. As many as twenty other works may be piled against yours. Although instructions are given to line paintings face-to-face and back-to-back to minimize damage, this isn't always done. To add to the problem, some shows require screw eyes and wires for hanging.

Your painting will be stacked until the jury convenes. Some societies judge on the same day, and others at a later date. Works are usually brought before the jury for review, judged, and restacked in accepted and rejected areas. The accepted works are reviewed for awards and once again stacked.

When a show closes, two methods are used to return works. A participant either removes his own painting off the wall, or a committee person searches through still another stack for the work.

What is the solution? You need to learn that group exhibition framing is distinctly different from assembling works for a solo show or a private collection. Place your works in moldings less susceptible to damage. There are sufficient styles available that by their very simplicity enhance rather than detract. Most media, oils excluded, benefit aesthetically from moderately sized, inconspicuous moldings. Furthermore, relying on basic materials such as plain wood, and colors such as black, and a combination of black and gold, rather than off-beat shades, makes restoration quick and easy. "Nordic" frames of hardwoods with rounded corners prevent chipping and splintering. Metal frames are available in both standard and canvas depths. (See Fig. 13 and Fig. 13a.)

Scouring flea markets for frames may be a good idea because of the astronomical rise in the price of raw lumber reflected in the cost of framing. Also check out garage sales and auctions.

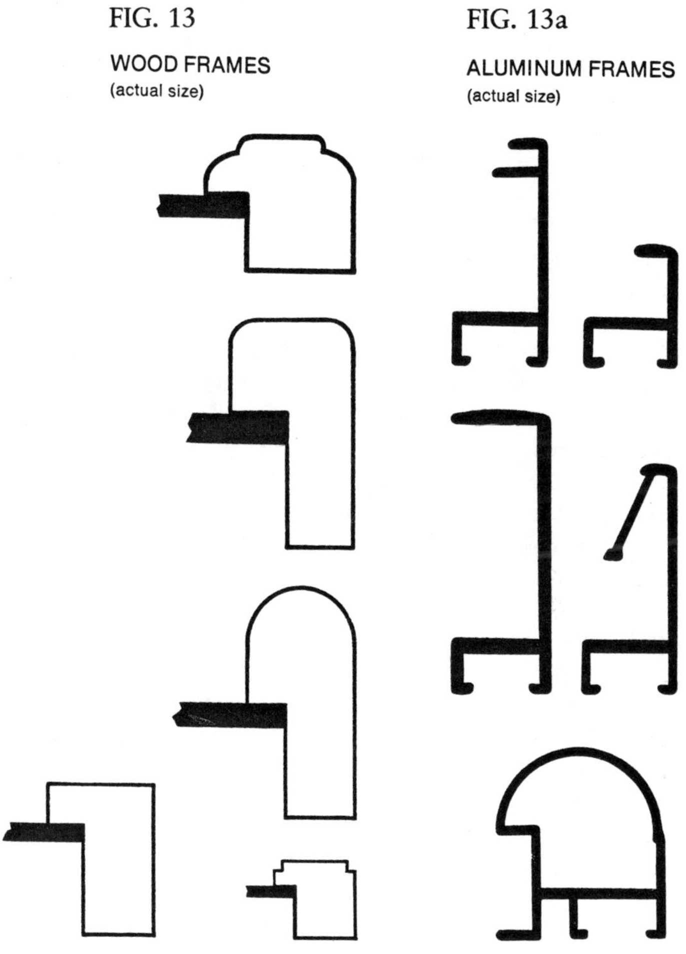
FIG. 13
WOOD FRAMES
(actual size)
FIG. 13a
ALUMINUM FRAMES
(actual size)

During one period in my career, I made frequent trips to a used furniture store hoping to discover collectible or antique objects. Surprisingly, I often uncovered an occasional frame or two. Sometimes, I would find an exquisite etching or lithograph. The proprietor and I also reached an understanding whereby I had first option on all prints, paintings, and frames I found there before they went to the auction block. Part of my studio was set aside for rejoining miters, repairing minor defects, refinishing surfaces, and scraping off dirt-encrusted glass.

This memorable experience coincided with my introduction to the sectional metal frame. Initially, it was treated with some reluctance by sponsoring organizations. But before long, metal frames became increasingly popular and kept pace with wood moldings—once viewed as sacrosanct—for glazed media. Now acceptable by most organizations, metal is both a blessing and curse, with distinct advantages and disadvantages.

Metal frames are relatively easy to assemble, requiring nothing more than a screwdriver. They are available either prepacked and sold in various retail outlets, or precut in standard or custom sizes and available through mail-order houses. Removing one end of the frame allows you to interchange works. Metal is more durable than wood and less susceptible to moisture, splitting and chipping, while also resistant to rust and stains.

On the other hand, metal frames get scratches and dents that are almost impossible to remove unless you're willing to replace one complete side. The glass in metal frames is vulnerable to breakage. Unlike a wood frame, rigidly supported by backing paper or cardboard, a metal frame is unbacked. Although rigid to a point, it has a tendency, especially in large sizes, to bow under its own weight when lifted by one side. This action separates the molding from the glass, causing a potential for damage when the frame is released.

There is one alternative if you prefer precut, do-it-yourself moldings. A recent innovation called "Frame-

Lok," a wood sectional frame, is available from Graphik Dimensions. Send for their free catalog.

Graphik Dimensions, Ltd.
Department AA, 41-23 Haight St.
Flushing, NY 11355
1-800-221-0262

This patented design is similar in assembly to metal frames and sold in pairs from 8″ to 48″ in 1″ increments. Other frame dealers are:

ASF American Frame Corporation
1340 Tomahawk Drive
Maumee, OH 43537
1-800-537-0944

The Frame Factory
760 W. Waveland Ave.
Chicago, IL 60613
1-800-621-6570 (free catalog)

Taylor Frame Company
13401 Sherman Way
North Hollywood, CA 91605
1-800-423-2620

Molding configurations, sizes, and materials are interrelated with matting and glazing. These three aspects of presenting a work need to meet organizational requirements. I suggest 100 percent rag museum board rather than matboard which tends to stain and discolor. Also, corrugated backing is not recommended against the subject unless a stain-free barrier is used between the two. Glazing, on the other hand, has become such a problem that many organizations forbid the use of regular glass.

The San Diego Watercolor Society states, *"Paintings must be framed with Plexiglas and simple gallery frames*

(30″ × 40″ max.). Matting if used must be white, off-white or neutral gray."—The American Watercolor Society plainly states, *"Frames must have plastic glazing."*—Iron Horse refuses metal frames without Plexiglas, and National Watercolor Society's travel show clause reads, *"To be eligible, paintings must be simply framed under Plexiglas or acrylic sheet and not exceed 30″ × 40″ including frame."*

The Kentucky Watercolor Society, Allied Artists of America, The Pastel Society, and Cooperstown Art Association all give you a choice—glass, acrylic, or Plexiglas.

Recent trends portend the eventual restriction of glass. Consider available alternatives. It's in your best interest to frame your works under nonglass materials for protection and to guarantee eligibility in any exhibition.

The Hudson River Museum's sixty-ninth Annual prospectus makes no mention of glazing requirements, but it clearly states other conditions: *"Paintings and graphics with wood frames must be wired with screw eyes facing the inside of the frame and not protruding from the frame. Metal section frames must be wired for hanging. Brackets should not be used to frame prints, drawings, or photographs. Unframed work on canvas with wood bracing must have all visible edges appropriately finished. Matted work will not be accepted."*

Hudson River Museum, like others, is forced by past, and still nagging, experiences to set out in detail framing requirements rarely found in any prospectus. Examine what you have put together and ask yourself, "Is this framing job good enough to hang in a museum?"

Another question you may be asking is, "Do I have the legal right to demand restitution from an exhibition sponsor?" Your submission to exhibit under the terms of the agreement absolves the organization of *"responsibility for loss or damage however caused in spite of every precaution in handling and protecting entries."* This statement, or a variation thereof, is found in almost every organizational prospectus.

Packing

Packing a work of art should be done right the first time. How you do it depends on a number of related factors—weight, size, subject configuration, and carrier requirements. These considerations dictate the choice of materials that are best suited to contain and protect your product. The aim is to cushion and isolate the work from moisture, torque, external forces, and mishandling. Fortunately, industry has developed devices and materials to transport large, heavy items thousands of miles. Although these commercial or industrial products may not vary individually in configuration as opposed to creative subject matter, the methods used to ship them are adaptable to any size, weight, and shape.

Moving vans crisscross the country transporting house furnishings, including framed works wrapped in blankets, with phenomenal success and with insurance available for replacement value. Itinerant artists transport dozens of works from state to state with apparently minimal protection but with maximum success.

With soft cushioning materials, rigid boards, wood that is virtually indestructible, synthetic glazing, and an application of good common sense, the once awesome task need no longer be faced with fear and trembling. Those who are unable to handle packing could use a professional crater or a local carpenter to assist them. Whether you do it yourself or have someone else handle the packing chores, remember that the items fabricated for this project are reusable packing materials. You'll be able to use them many times over in the years ahead.

Three-dimensional objects benefit mostly from limited size and weight, whereas "bigger and heavier" limits your choice in carriers. Also, keep in mind that you cannot surround a fifty-pound sculpture with shredded newspaper and expect it to remain intact.

There is a way to contain two- and three-dimensional works effectively to conform to carrier regulations and to survive shipping. This packing review will include a discussion of each of these aspects followed by illustrative specific case examples.

1. Available materials can be obtained from sources you encounter in everyday activity. Where you do business is your primary target. Other establishments will cooperate to establish good will and image in the community. Start with these potential providers:

Supermarket	*Corrugated boxes as containers; cut in sections for dividers. Drugs and notions or sundries partitioned cartons.*
Drugstore	*Same as supermarket*
Furniture Dealer	*Mattress containers for large corrugated sheeting.*
Appliance & TV Dealer	*Large, high-test corrugated cartons.*
Liquor Dealer	*Partitioned cartons for small three-dimensional items.*
Video, Computer & Electronic/Stereo Dealer	*High-test corrugated cartons, Styrofoam, polyfoam cushioning material.*
Floor Covering Dealer	*Heavyweight chipboard tubing for small three-dimensional items; also carpet remnants.*

2. Sources that supplement "free for the asking" material may require a cash outlay since not everything can be provided *gratis*. Although crate lumber can be had, warped boards are more of a headache than they are worth, and plywood or similar sheeting simply isn't

doled out like disposable cartons. Neither should you expect to be given large pieces of cushioning material. However, try these places to see what is available for a minimal cost:

Lumber Supply Outlet	*Plywood or other sheeting; wood boards; hardware.*
Craft Shop	*Poly batting; 100 percent bonded polyester; Styrofoam discs and rings.*
Fabric Shop	*Polyfoam sheeting.*

3. If you do not have the necessary tools, available space, inclination, or wherewithal to tackle packing, consider the professional crater. These companies are listed in the Yellow Pages under "Packing and Crating Service" or "Carpenters." In either case, provide accurate frame-size information, including whether or not screw eyes and wire are attached.

Discuss with a local carpenter construction methods and cost. Consider having several crates made at the same time in various sizes. Get a written estimate, if possible. Allow a reasonable length of time for completion. Of course, test the crate for fit before paying for it.

Since professional craters are experts in the field, they can be expensive. However, you may be pleasantly surprised to learn that a professionally made crate, twice or even three times the cost of anything else fabricated, will be less expensive in the long run. In the New York City metropolitan area contact:

Regency Worldwide Packing, Inc.
48-41 Van Dam Street
Long Island City, NY 11101
1/718-720-8877

My inquiry to David B. Epstein, President of Regency, elicited a gracious response along with a sincere effort to cooperate. He said, "Besides our packing facility, we have a modern, fireproof warehouse for the storage of art for both short and long term. The security system meets the latest standards for all the insurance companies, and we would be happy to quote rates on request.

"Because of the specific problems encountered in the specialized field we prefer not to quote general rates but are always happy to provide an estimate when given the proper information."

Write or call Regency for a crating specifications brochure.

The Art Carton Series, developed in 1980 by Pro-Pak, Inc., offers a somewhat different service for those unable to fabricate their own package but who are willing to do the packing and shipping. Designed to accommodate any art object no thicker than 2½ inches, the art carton kit concept provides a maximum of protection for any two-dimensional subject, including sculpture based on size limitations. Each kit includes—and I cite their literature:

1. A custom-sized carton made of strong, resilient double-wall corrugated fiberboard that telescopes to properly fit your objet d'art. The container's double-wall design provides five layers of protection (two layers of durable fiberboard, arches sealed between three sections of flat fiberboard). Each section is pre-sealed with staples resulting in a protective shell that's virtually impervious to damage.

2. Packing sheets of single-face corrugated fiberboard, light in weight and flexible enough to wrap around fragile items. This is used as a further protection against damage.

3. Sheets of DuPont Microfoam for use as an overwrap. Microfoam is a clean, white, soft-surface pad-

ding that protects items against abrasion and keeps out moisture, dust, and dirt. It can be cut, folded, and shaped to fit the object's contours and it provides a "selective friction" that clings to surfaces but does not scratch.

4. Easy-to-follow instructions for packing and shipping via United Parcel Service, bus, or any other carrier of your choice.

Kits are available in five sizes, ranging from 18"x18"x4" to 45"x40"x4" (all inside dimensions). However, Pro-Pak, Inc. will also fabricate reusable, custom, all-wood crates to your specifications and provide a quotation based on your requirements. For additional information write:

The Art Carton Series
P.O. Box 2282
Northbrook, IL 60062-9282
1-312-272-2684

These are but two examples. Such services are available in every part of the country. Check your phone directory for packers in your area. Remember, professionally made crates have a much longer life span, and their construction is more complicated than most of us are willing to tackle.

Example No. 1

You need to ship three miniature paintings, each measuring 5"x7" framed, with synthetic glazing. Combined, they assume an area 5¾"x7¾"x2", with a total weight of under two pounds. Considering these facts, packing materials are available almost anywhere—the supermarket, pharmacy, and your own house.

Method A

Place two to three inches of tightly crumpled newspaper on the bottom of a corrugated carton which should be four to six inches larger in all dimensions than the three works combined. Compress and add more paper if necessary; cover with a piece of corrugated material to fit snugly inside the carton; then compress the packing by hand.

Wrap each painting individually with paper toweling, tissue paper, or breathable plastic bags and center all three on the corrugated support sheet.

Surround completely with crumpled newspaper, compressed.

Cover with another piece of corrugated board, compressed.

Fill the carton with crumpled newspaper, close the flaps, and compress to test for *give*. Add more newspaper if necessary.

Tape down carton flaps.

Wrap in heavy brown kraft paper and seal. (Wrapping is forbidden by United Parcel Service but accepted by the United States Postal Service.) (See Fig. 14.)

FIG. 14 PACKING METHOD A

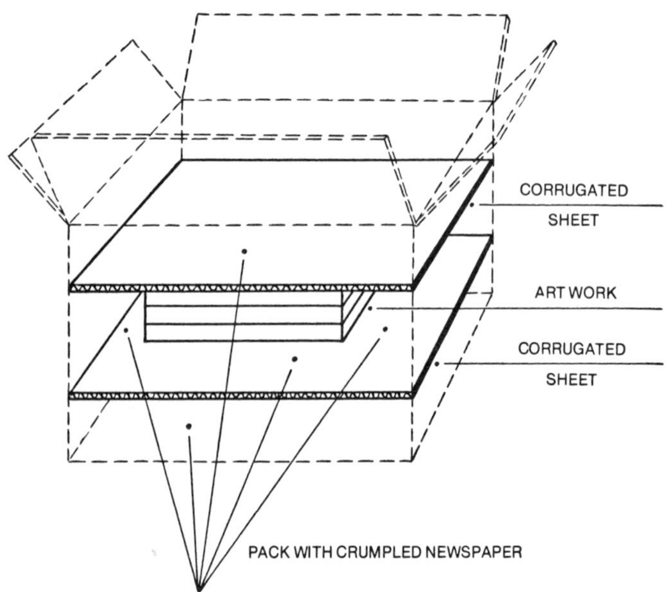

Method B

Using the same size carton and your three miniatures, place a 2″ thick pad of polyfoam on the bottom.

Center your individually wrapped miniatures over the polyfoam padding.

Fill in all four sides around the works with strips of polyfoam to the height of your paintings.

Cover with sufficient polyfoam padding to prevent rattling and seal the container. (See Fig. 15.)

FIG. 15 PACKING METHOD B

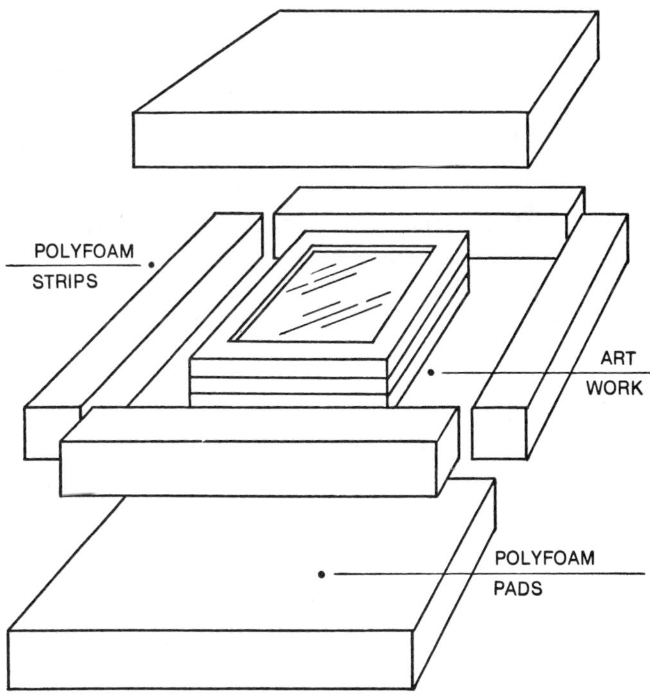

Method C

In spite of some reluctance to cushioning materials commonly called "chips" and "peanuts," their use can be quite effective in dealing with lightweight subjects, miniatures in particular. Merely surround your works with the "chips" or "peanuts" as you would with other cushioning materials to isolate the subjects. Prewrap your paintings as in methods A and B. I have shipped miniatures by this method many times with 100 percent success.

Example No. 2

Let's assume you need to transport a glazed work measuring 30″x24″ cross-country. You can construct your own crate or contract with someone else to do it. In either case, the construction's effectiveness is your responsibility, since no commercial packing firm guarantees against damage. The possibility of damage does exist based on handling and shipping methods, natural elements, and unavoidable accidents.

Faced with these possibilities, pack your work with adequate protective devices to reduce moisture penetration, shock, and frame damage. Enough material is available to support and protect. At the destination someone else will remove the contents, store the container, and later repack the work. Your painting's safety depends on:

a. Effective protection
b. Professional transportation
c. Ease of dismantling
d. Repacking
e. Return transportation

Statistics show that caution is exercised commensurate with the product's value. Artists have carted countless works in cars, vans, and trucks thousands of miles with makeshift protection without mishap. Should you expect less of those entrusted with your work?

Materials and Tools

1. Two sheets 1/4″ plywood or Masonite, 34″ × 28″
2. Construction quality boards 1″x4″ (actual size 3/4″x3 1/4″)x32″

3. Two construction quality boards 1″x4″ (actual size 3/4″x3 1/4″)x28″
4. Polyfoam padding
5. Paint
6. Rustproof nails and screws
7. Paintbrush
8. Hammer, saw, and screwdriver
9. Glue

First, a word about lumberyard practices. You may have to buy a full plywood sheet measuring 48″x96″. Unless your dealer will cut it for you, you must hand saw the required pieces. However, from one plywood sheet, you will get one extra 34″x28″ piece for use later. From two plywood sheets, you have enough to make three crates. (See Fig. 16.)

FIG. 16 PLYWOOD SHEET

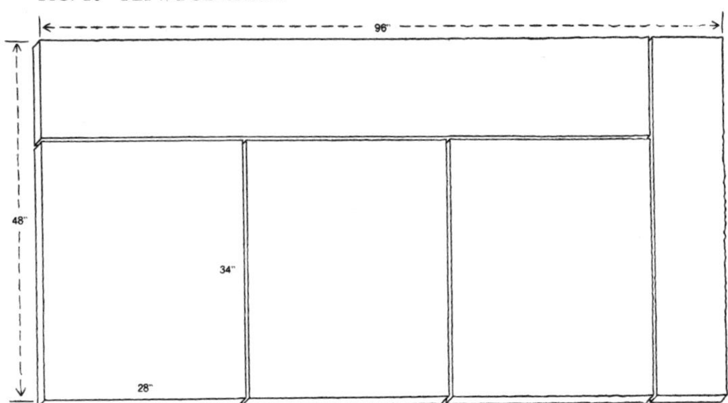

Second, a word about polyfoam. This soft, pliable, and durable material is an excellent cushioning device for separating objects and for wrapping. It is available in thicknesses 1/4″ to 6″ by 24″ wide to 78″ long. Polyfoam blocks measure 12″ by 12″ and 24″ by 24″ in thickness from 1/2″ to 6″. Check your Yellow Pages for fabric and upholstery stores that carry polyfoam remnants.

On a flat surface, loosely assemble all the sections, as illustrated in the bottom portion of Fig. 17, to check sizes and fit. Follow these ten easy steps: (See Fig. 17 and Fig. 17a.)

1. As a guide to be followed later, center your work on a plywood board. Trace in pencil the outline of the frame and remove.
2. Nail one 28″ board to the narrow end and two 32″ boards to the long sides of the board.
3. Cut and glue strips of polyfoam to three sides using the frame outline as a guide. The polyfoam should be equal to the depth of the frame.
4. Position frame between polyfoam strips—it should fit snugly.
5. Spot-glue sheet of polyfoam padding to one side of second plywood board. The padding must be slightly larger than the face of the frame and thick enough to occupy the remaining dead space.
6. Nail plywood to the three side boards. Counter-sink all nails and fill holes with wood putty (optional).
7. Stand crate on base and insert a loose polyfoam piece large enough to fill top cavity.
8. Position top board and drill enough holes to secure firmly. Use brass or rust resistant screws.
9. Paint completed crate for added moisture protection.
10. Add the following signs or cautions:
    a. Open This End
    b. Arrows to indicate top
    c. Stem glass—Fragile (optional)
    d. Umbrella—Keep Dry (optional)

FIG. 17 WOOD CRATE CONSTRUCTION

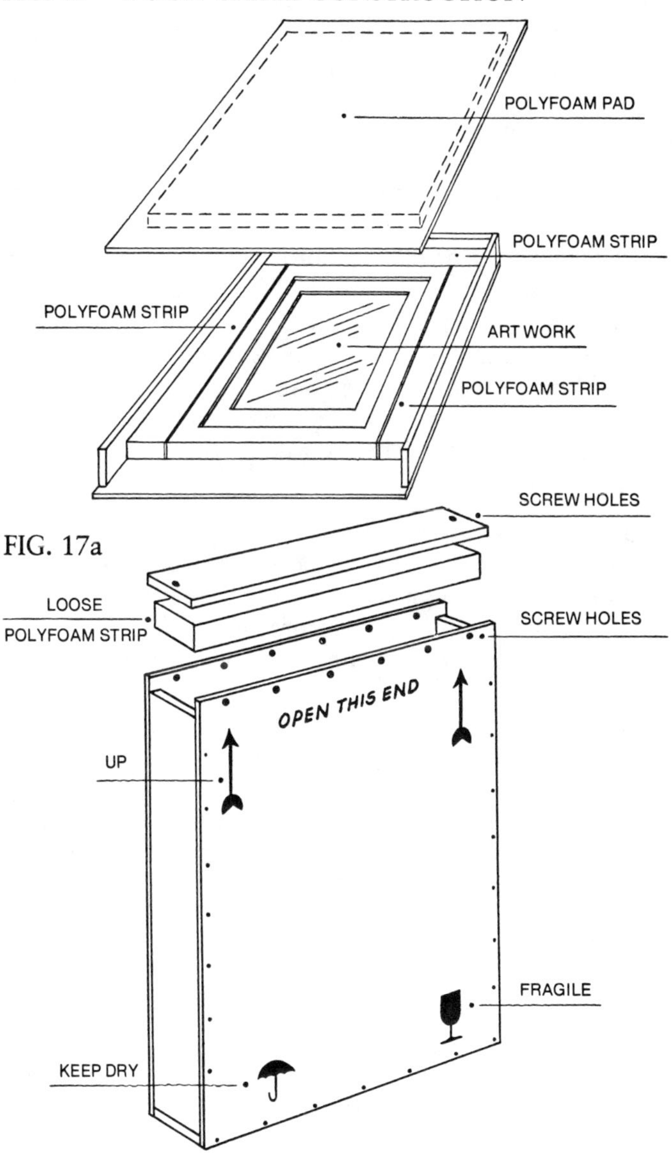

FIG. 17a

This crate is suitable for all framed work. Heavier cushioning material is advisable with oils framed with wood strips which allow minimum protection against canvas puncture. Corrugated corner protectors are also advisable with strip framing. Make your own or purchase them precut and prescored from your local art supplies dealer or from the Graphik Dimensions, Ltd. catalog.

Matted works do not require a crate. My favorite method is to use a sheet of 1/4″ Masonite board (use a damp cloth to clean off residue before packing) as a stiffener. Wrap your works in paper. Cut two sheets of corrugated board slightly larger than the Masonite and seal on all four sides. The most common problem with flat corrugated packaging is bent corners. Masonite prevents the condition.

Example No. 3

Three-dimensional objects are no less exempt from potential hazards than glazed works and canvas. Whereas two-dimensional objects are protected by wood, corrugated board, polyfoam padding and blocks, sculpture requires the use of less compressible materials such as Styrofoam and wood. Any soft material to fill in large cavities surrounding a piece of sculpture would give way under the weight.

A sandstone head, sitting on a pedestal in my dining room, measures 17″ high, 8″ wide, and 9″ deep and weighs fifty-one *pounds*. If carelessly packed, this piece would crush a cardboard carton. Small, fragile, and lightweight objects may be wrapped in soft material and placed in a divided liquor carton. If possible, leave the outer carton spaces empty to act as an air barrier between the works and external pressure.

To ship a 20-pound sculpture (an average weight for small works) follow these simple steps: (See Fig. 18.)

1. Outline the subject, either standing or lying flat, on two equally sized large Styrofoam blocks.

2. With a sharp knife and peeler/corer kitchen tool, carve out a cavity larger than half the object in each block.
3. Wrap the artwork in a soft, protective material and position between the two sections of carved Styrofoam.
4. Remove more Styrofoam, if necessary. Larger cavities are better than a tight fit. Any play or unnecessary tendency to movement is resolved with additional cushioning material.

FIG. 18 PACKING SCULPTURE

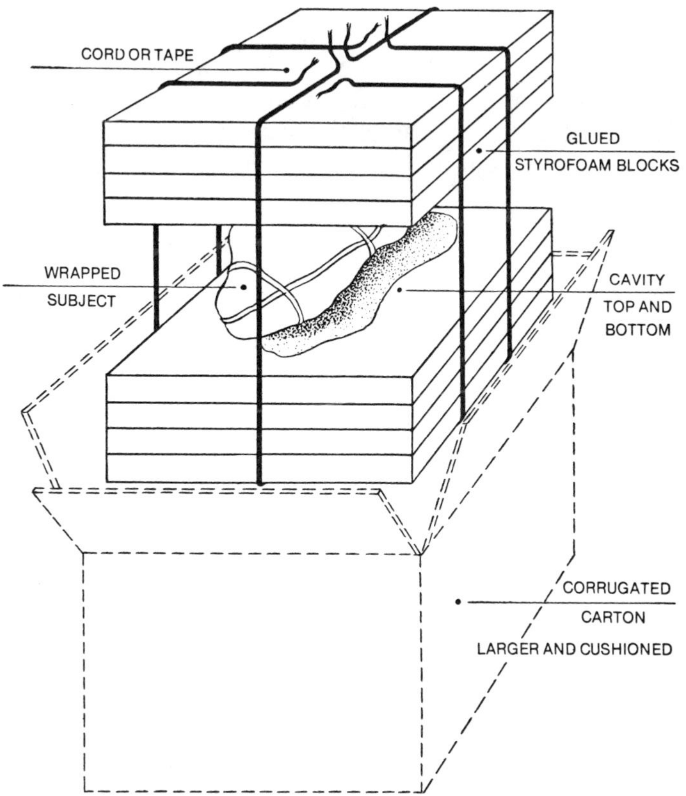

5. Tie the two blocks with twine or secure with untearable tape.
6. Place in a corrugated box and fill in empty spaces with corrugated pads or polyfoam.

(Note: Styrofoam provides adequate protection and can be shipped via some carriers when wrapped in heavy paper and taped.)

The outer carton with its fillers adds another measure of safety. If adequately sized Styrofoam blocks are unavailable, simply combine and glue together several pieces to the desired size.

Similarly small items can be cushioned and shipped in old typewriter, luggage, and other rigid cases. Tie or tape securely.

Although some organizations do not accept three-dimensional works, many do. Some impose weight and size limitations, and some do not. When the prospectus fails to include these limitations, the organization is bound by implied agreement to accept any size work passing the jury of selection.

Organizations that do impose limitations are usually specific. For instance, both Audubon Artists and Allied Artists place a dimensional restriction of 24″x34″x80″ (in the round) and a weight limitation of 300 pounds.

The North American Sculpture Exhibition at the Foothills Art Center in Golden, Colorado, limits a work of sculpture to 125 cubic feet or 500 pounds.

These organizations show great consideration and generosity in providing opportunities for the sculptor. But a 300- or 500-pound sculpture is not a common exhibitable work and requires packaging and shipping methods best left to the professional. Commercial carriers are equipped to move, protect, and transport even the most fragile of large items.

Shipping

Limitations imposed by sponsoring organizations on size

and weight play a lesser role than shipping restrictions. Compare and correlate the two, and know that the carrier, not the organization, establishes the ultimate shipping guidelines. Furthermore, you cannot submit anything unless you know the shipping carriers' allowances. I suggest, therefore, that you prepare and submit your entry based on the following facts:

a. National organizations accept shipped and hand-delivered works.

b. These organizations consider the ease and limited expense of those able and willing to exhibit.

c. Size and weight limitations favor hand delivery.

d. Size and weight limitations of shipped entries include packing materials.

The primary carriers are:

1. The United States Postal Service
2. Greyhound Package Express
3. United Parcel Service (UPS)

All three are reliable. Familiarize yourself with the requirements of each so you can then decide which system best suits your needs. But before you decide, check the prospectus since some organizations have a preference or may forbid the use of a particular carrier.

1. United States Postal Service

The Post Office accepts any artwork adquately packaged but limited to seventy pounds. Its insurance covers any amount *with certain stipulations*. When the insured value exceeds $400, a package must be sent by registered mail. Ask for a return receipt request to be signed by the recipient and then returned to you. This assures you that your work has arrived at its destination, identifies the recipient, and tells you how long it took for the package to get there—a helpful clue for use in future shipments.

The Postal Service does not have a pickup service.

However, in some areas a carrier will pick up small items from your mailbox and bring you the itemized charges the next day. The Postal Service performs many similar and convenient services, particularly in suburban and rural areas, but it is not equipped to pick up a large work.

2. Greyhound Package Express

Greyhound will not accept works framed with glass. It will transport three-dimensional objects and subjects under Plexiglas or acrylic, if adequately packaged. In contrast to the United States Postal Service, Greyhound will pick up at your home if you live in a large metropolitan area. The fee is $4 within city limits and $5 in outlying areas. Check with your nearest Greyhound facility for information on the availability of this service. For delivery or pickup at destination, advance and specific arrangements must be made with Greyhound before sponsoring organizations can pick up your work. One condition to be met—but not critical—is Greyhound's insurance coverage limitations: $500 intrastate and $1,000 interstate.

3. United Parcel Service (UPS)

The United Parcel Services brochure, *Package With Care,* is a handy reference guide suggesting packing materials to use, methods of internal protection, proper sealing, and labeling. It also has a graphically illustrated section on "Packaging No-Nos." The brochure is available at your local UPS office. Some quotes from it follow:

> *You don't have to be a packaging expert to protect your shipment . . . Common, readily available materials can provide adequate cushioning for almost any item.*
>
> *One of the best methods is to use the paper from heavy brown grocery bags, crumpled and stuffed around the item to be shipped. If bags are not available crumpled sheets of newspaper are*

> *the next best choice . . . It is very important to pack several inches of your cushioning material in the bottom of the carton. Then, wrap each item separately and place them in the center of the carton. Now, stuff cushioning material firmly around and between the items.*

UPS applies its packing suggestions to items of reasonable size and weight. Remember what I have already said about sculpture, and use the packing methods as described.

Glazed works are accepted under specific conditions. No wooden crates are allowed. The outer container of a package must be 4″ larger on all sides than the inner container. UPS is not concerned with packing aesthetics; it will accept a corrugated carton regardless of the surface printing matter.

UPS also recommends the following:

> *To close a carton securely, use a strong tape—2″ or more in width—such as the tapes described below.*
>
> *PRESSURE SENSITIVE PLASTIC. Generally, the easiest, most convenient to use. It is quite versatile because it will adhere without water, and can stick to a variety of surfaces and shapes.*
>
> *WATER ACTIVATED PAPER TAPE. Use a minimum of 3″ width for carton sealing, of the grade known as 60-pound tape. You will need to apply 3 strips of tape to both top and bottom of the carton . . .*

UPS stresses several important labeling points:

> *Place the delivery label on the top of the carton. ("Top" should be the most stable orientation of the package as it might ride on a conveyor.)*

> *Place no other address label on the carton.*
> *Do not place the label over a seam or closure, or on top of sealing tape.*
> *Remove or cross out any old address labels or markings on a used carton.*
> *For added protection, place a duplicate label or other delivery information copy inside of your package.*

A $100 insurance cap is placed on artwork unless a greater value can be substantiated. However, whether authentication other than a certified appraisal is sufficient in the event of a claim is questionable. In the event of a loss, proof must be provided in the form of a print or picture of the artwork. UPS is controlled by Interstate Commerce Commission (ICC) regulations which require justification for paying higher claims.

Resolving this problem isn't easy. Blanket appraisals aren't allowed, and you wouldn't want to have each work appraised individually because of the cost. But neither should you be denied the services offered by UPS because of this restriction. One resolution is discussed in the next chapter.

An important feature of UPS is their unlimited home pickup service with a $3.25 weekly charge. Call at least one day in advance, indicate weight and size of your package, yours and the receiver's name and address, and insurance required. (The $100 cap still applies.) The charges will be given to you by phone to be paid in cash or check at time of pickup. The driver will give you a receipt. Additionally,

> *When UPS picks up a package, the shipper may prepare a stamped, self-addressed Acknowledgment of Delivery form and attach it to the package. A signature is obtained at the time of delivery, and the form is returned to the address*

specified by the shipper. A small additional charge is assessed for each Acknowledgment of Delivery.

The review of the three carriers contains factors which may have a bearing on your preference. Study the chart to make a decision. (See Fig. 19.)

FIG. 19 CARRIER REQUIREMENTS

CARRIER	ART ACCEPTED	MAXIMUM WEIGHT	MAXIMUM SIZE	AVAILABLE INSURANCE
U.S. POSTAL SERVICE	NO RESTRICTIONS	70 POUNDS	108" MAXIMUM — COMBINED LENGTH AND GIRTH	*NO LIMIT
GREYHOUND PACKAGE EXPRESS	WITH RESTRICTIONS	100 POUNDS	141" MAXIMUM — COMBINED LENGTH AND GIRTH	$500 MAXIMUM INTRASTATE $1,000 MAXIMUM INTERSTATE
UNITED PARCEL SERVICE	WITH RESTRICTIONS	70 POUNDS	108" MAXIMUM — COMBINED LENGTH AND GIRTH	$100 FREE INSURANCE 25¢ EACH ADDITIONAL $100 **NO LIMIT

*The Postal service will insure an object for any amount based on verification of value and the discretion of the postmaster.

**UPS will do the same if authentication of value is provided by a certified, written appraisal in advance of shipment. Otherwise, the $100 cap is in force.

Costs and travel time are based on where you live, availability of service, and your ability to get to the service facility. Some carriers are willing to come to you if you are willing to pay the fee. The cost comparison chart contains information that tells you the ultimate destination of your shipment. It is your responsibility to know if this meets an organization's policy stand. (See Fig. 20.) The time factor is relevant only if you procrastinate in shipping a work.

FIG. 20 COST COMPARISON CHART

* 20 POUNDS SHIPPED FROM TAMPA, FLORIDA TO SEATTLE, WASHINGTON

CARRIER	TRAVEL TIME	SHIPPING METHOD	COST	$400 INSURANCE	EXTRAS	TOTAL COST
U.S. Postal Service	3-5 Days	Post Office To Destination	$21.41	$4.70	$3.60 Registered Mail Fee	$29.71
Greyhound Package Express	4 Days	Terminal To Terminal	$27.00	$1.00	$4.00 Optional Pick-up Fee	$32.00
United Parcel Service	6 DAYS	Door-To-Door Delivery	$10.83	$.75	$3.25 Home Pick-up Fee	$14.83

* ESTIMATE COSTS FROM YOUR POINT OF ORIGIN TO DESTINATION

Other Services

Overnight delivery services, air cargo, and motor freight carriers fail to meet the tests of accessibility and reasonable cost. But, they are sometimes necessary alternatives because of the need to transport oversize and overweight objects. In these instances bear in mind that your container must withstand the stresses of being hoisted by mechanical lifting devices and also be able to support the weight of heavy crates. Your work must be delivered to an air terminal. This adds to your shipping cost. A motor freight company will transport any size and weight crate at relatively reasonable cost, but buy insurance elsewhere.

Many artists and sculptors create works requiring these special shipping services (sculptors in particular). Consult the Yellow Pages for a listing of these carriers.

Organizational Requirements

Each organization determines its own policies for size of works and shipping methods based on ease of control, limited involvement, available space, and manpower. Some accept direct shipping, while many direct all entries to an off-site location. A few examples follow:

The National Watercolor Society in California designates a professional crating and shipping company to handle all works. It also advises which shipping services it does and does not recommend. The prospectus states:

> *Entries must be shipped prepaid, addressed to Cooke's (see above). Return will be made by same carrier collect, plus a charge for unpacking and repacking. Write or call Cooke's for information on specific charges. Ship early, notify Cooke's on date of shipment and carrier. Include registry fee. ($6.00 per painting.)*
>
> *Note: Do not ship by bus, as that necessitates an expensive pick-up and return at the busline, charged to the shipper. UPS, U.S. Mail, Air Freight, and Motor Freight will accept framed and glazed paintings for shipment.*

The NWS provides specific and useful information often omitted in a prospectus. (The reference to Cooke's, of course, indicates NWS' receiving and shipping agent. The prospectus gives information on shipping to Cooke's, and its address elsewhere.)

Butler Institute of American Art states in part:

> *Paintings will be returned shipping charges collect via the same means they were sent, unless Butler Institute is notified otherwise. Artists who send work PARCEL POST ARE REQUIRED TO MAIL A LIKE AMOUNT OF THE CHARGE to Butler Institute before the work can be returned. U.S. Mail cannot be shipped collect.*

Butler requires a letter of authorization when the artist

requests a return shipment which differs from the original method and concludes that COD is not acceptable by U.S. mail. However, if the artist's authorization specifies "return COD," the Postal Service will accept such documentation for collecting postage and insurance from the receiver. In the unlikely event the artist refuses his own painting, it is returned to the sender.

Major metropolitan New York art organizations suggest the service of:

Berkeley Express Company
27 Vestry Street
New York, NY 10013
1-212-226-6788

As with all qualified agents, Berkeley imposes certain requirements to allow for on-time delivery of your work and to avoid any unnecessary surcharges. Note the following:

1. Berkeley will not pick up from the airport.
2. Works must arrive at least two days in advance of the day of delivery to the sponsoring organization.
3. No soft cartons, e.g., corrugated or cardboard, will be accepted.
4. Works must be shipped to Berkeley prepaid and returned collect.
5. Works shipped by bus and not delivered to the Berkeley warehouse will be assessed $12 for pickup and return.
6. Work sent by UPS will be returned prepaid in some cases, and the charges billed to the artist.
7. Berkeley accepts delivery from any carrier provided you meet their packaging requirements, and your work is delivered on time.

For a complete listing of Berkeley's requirements and a schedule of charges, write to them at the above address.

Art organizations that rely on agents such as Berkeley

to uncrate, deliver, recrate, and return your works are, in essence, providing a service for you in spite of the charge involved. Berkeley employs professionals trained in the use of the essential equipment to protect and store fragile material.

When a group applies size limitations, it's performing a service by informing you that certain numbers may be in excess of most carrier regulations.

Hand Delivery

We cannot discuss shipping artwork without including hand delivery. Certain protective considerations, similar to those used by shippers, must be considered when loading artwork into your own vehicle.

Loading artwork into the trunk of your vehicle simulates putting an object in a shipping container. Unfinished metal areas, protrusions, and dead space are tantamount to the problems you try to avoid with a hand-fabricated crate. When subjected to the vehicle's constant motion, braking, accelerating, and less than ideal road surface conditions, your work risks being damaged if you fail to provide protection for it. Use any material available to cushion and prevent motion and rubbing problems. Place two or more framed pieces face-to-face and back-to-back. Support a three-dimensional object to avoid toppling.

Placing works on the back seat is not only hazardous for the object but for the driver and passengers as well. Small three-dimensional objects, therefore, are best placed on the floor. Stand framed works, only when absolutely necessary, on the floor in the back.

There should be a correlation between the trunk compartment and the size of your works. A vehicle with limited storage area will almost force you to create smaller images. Consider the problem when you purchase a vehicle. A case in point:

Before purchase I examined every station wagon with a measuring tape to see if it would accommodate the largest work I could transport. When it could not do so, I looked elsewhere for one that would. Once, good judgment and common sense failed me completely. Struck by the overall impact of a Pontiac Grand Prix, my wife and I, minus our tape, agreed we were on safe ground looking at a trunk that seemed enormous in size. So, we bought the car.

Soon thereafter, we picked up some paintings delivered by an artist friend. No matter how hard I tried, the trunk would not accommodate my largest work. Somehow I managed to squeeze it into the area between the front and back seat. Unfortunately, we were left with an extra passenger who had nowhere to sit. I later traded the Grand Prix with its apparently large trunk for a medium-size station wagon.

When we relocated to Florida, over twenty paintings were loaded in the cargo area and protected during the 1,100 mile trip by using thin blankets, corrugated sheets, and space fillers to prevent rattling and shifting.

Smaller imports and domestic wagons have limited space but usually provide enough storage capacity for moderately sized works. Vans are ideal for large works and can accommodate great numbers. It is wise to consider potential problems you *might* face in hand deliveries based on the size of your vehicle to your works. During the early stages of your career, work patterns and size preferences will automatically develop. Unless your vehicle can accommodate overly large pieces, you will either have to maintain a disciplined production regimen or, occasionally, rent a vehicle to transport your larger pieces.

Questions

Q. How do you clean Plexiglas or acrylic?

A. Incorrect methods can cause damaged glazing. Follow these instructions carefully:

1. Use K-Lux Safe T-Vue Plastic Cleaner, Magic Plastic Window Cleaner in a spray can, but DO

NOT USE WINDEX.
2. Wipe clean with a dry, lint-free cloth. Coarse paper towels scratch the surface.
3. An alternate method is to use a 1 percent solution of mild dishwashing liquid detergent and water. Wipe dry with soft cotton flannel or jersey cloth.
4. Remove grease, paint, or tar with a varnish and painter's VMP naphtha.
5. An occasional thin application of quality auto paste wax (not cleaner/wax combination) will fill in most surface scratches and help maintain a lustre. Buff with a soft flannel rag.
6. Do not use leaded or ethyl gas, concentrated alcohol, benzene, acetone, lacquer thinners, or carbon tetrachloride.

Q. *Where do you purchase framing materials?*

A. I've run the gamut from buying lumberyard moldings, mitering, finishing, and assembling the sections, to cutting mats and glass. On other occasions I have just cut a mat and assembled all the components.

There's no absolute way except that which is most comfortable for you and easiest on your wallet. Consider buying finished frames from a variety of retail outfits, or check any art magazine for mail-order houses. Precut mats are available.

Q. *Why do organizations prefer and advise using certain carriers over others?*

A. Many organizations either have a working arrangement with a specific carrier or have developed policies based on past experiences.

Q. *What do you think of nonglare glass?*

A. In spite of acceptance in some quarters, nonglare glass has limitations and should be used sparingly, if at all. To avoid image distortion and diffusion, it should be placed directly against the subject matter. Since nonglare glass is merely acid treated glass, direct contact could pose a problem unless the acid residue is washed off. In any event, glass of any kind is slowly being disallowed by more and more organizations.

Q. *Is colored matting acceptable?*

A. Experience will show that where matting is necessary, the ultimate purpose is to isolate the subject from external distractions by providing a subtle, nonintrusive separation. Color defeats that purpose.

Q. *Why can't I send my work directly to the art association instead of to a crating and shipping agent?*

A. An art association establishes policy that refines its procedures. An agent unpacks, stores, crates, and transports works ready to be hung. When a show closes, the agent picks up, repacks, and ships works at your expense. This way the association eliminates the need for additional manpower, storage space, and shipping.

Q. *Is shipping a work by registered mail a good idea?*

A. You may pay extra, but your work will receive special attention from the point of departure to the recipient. With registered mail you must declare the value of the work, whether you insure it or not, but insurance is advisable. Your receipt is a valuable document in the event of damage or loss. It is the best protection you can buy for the money.

Q. *What about certified mail?*

A. Certified mail is worthwhile because it provides evidence of shipment. Delivery to the recipient's post office is recorded and maintained for tracking purposes. However, since certified mail is used for objects only of intrinsic—not commercially appraisable—value, insurance is not available.

Chapter 7

INSURANCE AND LIABILITY

In any agreement where goods are exchanged the responsibilities, inherent rights, and extent of recourse of both sender and receiver are defined. A prospectus includes factors that closely resemble such a document. It is to your advantage to learn the full meaning of those quasi-legal conditions that may well stand up in litigation proceedings. I don't mean to imply that such action is a probability. But it is important to discuss facts often misunderstood.

To a creative person, the requirements, limitations, restrictions, warnings, and general legalese in a prospectus may seem merely academic. But you'll find that there are many questions to be answered. For example:

Why is an entry fee necessary and how is it used?

Is there any guarantee of protection when a work is submitted, accepted, and displayed? Is insurance essential?

Who is to blame if a work is slightly damaged, destroyed, stolen, or lost?

Fees

An entry fee is a basic requirement for involvement and varies in amount from one organization to another.

Acceptance alone justifies remitting the fee, without which there can be no exposure. Combine this with a potential for monetary and merchandise awards and you soon realize that the system is indeed worth the gamble. It's here where we find the clue to how collected fees are spent.

Funds are used primarily to guarantee the survival of the effort. Without donations from organization members, well-wishers, and dedicated art patrons, many groups would be forced to struggle to meet costs, such as the following:

a. Paid announcements in art magazines;
b. Design, type matter, photostats, and printing of the prospectus;

c. Mailing costs of the prospectus;
d. Jury fees (not applicable in some cases);
e. Mailing costs of jury results (not applicable in some cases);
f. Awards, medals, ribbons, and certificates;
g. Design, type matter, awards reproductions, and printing of exhibition catalog (not applicable in some cases);
h. Rental space (not applicable in some cases);
i. Advertisements (not applicable in some cases).

Many organizations survive on membership dues, limited sales commissions, and endowments.

Southeastern Watercolorists II states in its prospectus, *A portion of the funding for this project has been provided through a grant from the Institute of Museum Services, a Federal agency.*

Mainsail Arts Festival operates under the sponsorship of the City of St. Petersburg Department of Leisure Services, the Arts Center of St. Petersburg, and the Junior League of St. Petersburg, Florida.

Butler Institute of American Art functions with the support of the Ohio Arts Council.

These are representative examples showing how two museums and a major outdoor festival are partially funded by a municipal agency and an arts council's support.

Insurance

Some insurance companies offer services directly related to your creative output. Are your works insurable? Yes, by methods requiring systematic premium payments with a supportive policy containing inclusions and exclusions. Commercial insurance is not your only recourse to guaranteed protection. First, let's look at a report of historical significance which dates back to the middle of the 19th century. It was found in the *Art Journal for 1878.*

> *But the most important subject which the Congress* (Art-Congress at Antwerp, Belgium) *has had under debate was that of international copyright in works of art. It will be remembered that in the year 1858 the Brussels Congress strongly supported the claims of artists to protection from piracy, but, although this principle was triumphantly carried, and the Brussels assembly, composed, as it was, of the most eminent artists and jurists, sought from time to time to establish on solid bases the public guarantees of copyright, their efforts in this direction remained without any effectual results. The Antwerp Congress of 1861, again met with but little better success; for although eight European governments sent representatives to this gathering and the Congress drew up a formula of principles circumscribing the laws of copyright or ownership in works of art within just limits, and fixing the period when society could and ought to exercise its rights of claiming the resignation of proprietorship for public benefit, their report remained a dead letter. It is to be hoped that the labours of the Antwerp Congress of 1877 will be better rewarded; at present the rights of artists are no better secured than they were in 1861.*

Does the subject of copyright, spoken simultaneously with common insurance, come as a surprise? As critical as premium insurance may be, automatic protection against plagiarism of your work, provided by the copyright laws of the U.S. government, is just as far-reaching. The Copyright Revision Act of 1976 automatically negated the 1909 Copyright Statute which transferred the copyright from the seller to the purchaser. Under the new law the buyer owns the creative work only and loses the right to exploit its use for monetary gain. Print editions, mass reproductions in any form, or any similar commercial use is forbidden. The artist retains his inalienable right to the mass exploitation of his work unless a mutual and written agreement to the contrary is concluded between the artist and buyer.

Why has protection for the artist and his work resisted legislative enactment and enforcement for such a long time? Why did it take sixty-seven years to revise a statute which left an artist vulnerable to having his works plagiarized? In truth, the artist may have been the major culprit, being preoccupied primarily with creative interests rather than joining forces with other artists to establish a united front. Deep involvement with aestheticism left little room for pragmatism until concerned groups formulated aggressive policies against injustices and exploitation. Organizations dedicated to the interests of the art community solicit member support of legislation pending in the United States Congress by providing incentive methods for bombarding their representatives with written opinions, pro and con; *Vox Populi!* The voice of the people!

By copyrighting your work, you are warning the world against any infringement of your rights; you are stating that you will protect them, and that you are backed by the support of the U.S. government. But, this warning is only a temporary measure meant to alert would-be offenders that you are cognizant of your legal rights.

In the event of infringement of the Copyright Act, you are required to set protective machinery in motion by officially registering the plagiarized work before the three-month grace period of protection ends. Forms and a Copyright Information Kit are available from:

Register of Copyrights
Library of Congress
Washington, DC 20559

You must state the nature of your work, provide photographs or copies from a printed edition, and remit a small fee. In turn you will receive an official certificate of registration to provide the ammunition needed in litigation proceedings against the offender.

This two-step method was devised to preclude the need to register officially and to pay a fee for every piece of work produced until the need presented itself. Nevertheless, the option to do so is yours.

What about other protection? Are your artworks covered against loss, damage, or total destruction? Are the works you ship protected, and does the sponsoring organization insure them while on its premises? Why do some organizations photograph and reproduce your entry without permission? These questions, and more, will be answered when we discuss homeowners or renters insurance, personal articles policy, and carrier insurance. The combination of these coverages provides more than adequate protection at a surprisingly low cost.

Homeowners or Renters Insurance

Whether you rent or own your home, insurance protection for your possessions is available. A renter is not required to have insurance but a homeowner, whose property is mortgaged, is required by the lending institution to insure the physical or real property to the extent of the mortgage amount. Although insuring the value of the contents of a house is optional, a homeowners or renters policy is usually written to insure both structure and contents. The policy offers you the opportunity to insure your artworks in part or as a whole. More insurance means more protection. For instance:

a. Let's assume you insure the contents of your premises for $20,000.

b. By your estimate, the works in your studio work area are worth $12,000.

c. A fire consumes your studio and an adjoining room.

d. Works of art, studio equipment, and household property are destroyed beyond recovery.

e. An insurance claims adjuster reviews the damage to determine the loss.

f. It is concluded that the fire was accidental and not intentional.

A settlement is reached. It includes the total value of all your works and household property, less its normal depreciation. If you want full reimbursement for household items, your policy must include a replacement clause. There is an additional premium for this clause which has no bearing on original works of art. Since art does not depreciate, you can expect full compensation for any loss based on conditions to be described later. However, the total claim cannot exceed the coverage limit purchased.

Additional protection for artwork in your possession, during shipping, and while on exhibition is available provided you meet certain criteria. Called a Personal Articles Policy (PAP) and commonly known as a fine arts floater, it can be bought separately or together with the homeowners or renters insurance.

Personal Articles Policy (PAP)

A PAP provides supplemental protection for valuable possessions including fine art. For an artist it is probably the wisest insurance investment available, provided you are ready to abide by certain requirements and conditions.

The low cost is a bargain in view of what it does—in-home protection, during shipment, while on exhibition, and return shipping. The insurance company makes the ground rules, and eligibility is based on compliance as follows:

1. Who you are, where and how you live, your reputation in the community, financial resources, and credit rating, all have a bearing on the risk assumed by a company.

a. Art collections to be insured require some safeguards against potential damage or loss. Converted barn studios, trailer parks, multitenanted complexes, and old run-down frame houses all pose fire and burglary risks. Deadbolt locks, smoke and fire detectors, fire extinguishers, and security systems are questionable safeguards under such conditions. These restrictions are based on sound insurance policies fortified by statistical data.

b. Another question to be resolved is the extent of your creative involvement. Is your main source of income derived from art? Do sales of your work only supplement income from some other full-time vocation? Is creativity a commercial venture or hobby? If your major or only source of income is based on art activity, you may not be eligible under the personal article policy but insurable in some other way, i.e., business insurance. Historically, a fine arts floater was designed to protect primarily collectors of fine art rather than exhibiting artists. But coverage expanded over a period of time to include much broader terms.

c. All insurance policies describe how and when you are covered and how and when you are not. These descriptions detail at great length precise examples of conditions that determine your claims. A primary exclusion that will affect you reads as follows: *This form does not insure against loss or damage to property on exhibition at fairgrounds or premises at national or international expositions unless endorsed hereon.*

This clause makes certain that you inform the insurance company that your art is to be exhibited, and a policy will be underwritten accordingly at a higher rate. This increased premium is not prohibitive considering the higher risk of damage and loss in outdoor exhibitions.

2. Aside from all this, the main purpose of a fine arts floater is to differentiate between the total contents

of a home as covered by homeowners or renters insurance and specifically itemized items. You are not automatically insured for $10,000 worth of works unless you complete and submit a personal articles schedule with the insurance company. This schedule lists, describes, and evaluates each work to be insured, and only those so itemized are covered against loss or damage. (See Fig. 21.)

FIG. 21 FINE ARTS FLOATER SCHEDULE

ITEM NUMBER	DESCRIPTION	LIMIT OF LIABILITY
1	"ROCKS" - ROCKS, TREES, WATER, W.C.	$1000.00
2	"WILCOX POINT" - BEACH + TREES FROM OCEAN - W.C.	550.00
3	"CLEARING" - AUTUMN LANDSCAPE - W.C.	600.00
4	"NUDE FIGURE" - MARBLE TORSO — SCULPTURE	300.00
5	"WINTER MORNING" - HOUSES, SNOW, SKY - W.C.	1000.00
6	"FLORAL" - FLOWERS IN VASE - W.C.	200.00
7	"ECCE HOMO" - HEAD OF JESUS - SANDSTONE	500.00

a. The liability limit is the value of your works, substantiated by data such as past sales, exhibition catalog prices, commercial gallery affiliation, or by professional appraisal.

b. A fine arts floater, like most agreements, contains conditions which may affect a claim for loss or damage and, unless followed to the letter, may render the policy ineffective. Falsifying, misrepresenting, and concealing facts or the circumstances relating to the insurance and/or claim may void the policy.

c. The law of your resident state takes precedence over the policy provisions when in conflict.

d. The "schedule" is not a rigid and unalterable document. At any time you may add or delete works to the original list. However you alter the fine arts schedule, either above or below the original

$10,000 mentioned, your premium rate will change—higher or lower.

As your reputation grows, so will the price of your product, necessitating revisions in your schedule. Such alterations can be made but only in writing to the company. Any increase in the total liability limit will mean an additional premium.

It is important to keep in mind that although the fine arts floater and homeowners or renters insurance are separate documents, they are interrelated. The floater establishes a basis for the value of other works not scheduled and kept in your flat drawer file or closet and protected by either homeowners or renters insurance. In the hypothetical studio fire, a claims adjuster accepted the value placed on the destroyed works based on the liability limits data found in the fine arts floater.

These conditions are not difficult to work through, since all conditions do not apply simultaneously. Professional advice is available. The following companies all offer fine arts coverage:

1. State Farm Insurance Companies
2. The Atlantic Companies
3. Chubb and Son, Inc.
4. Insurance Company of North America (CIGNA)
5. Marine Office of America Corp.
6. Fireman's Fund Insurance Co.
7. St. Paul and Marine Insurance Co.
8. The Travelers Companies

These companies have exemplary reputations. If their services do not meet your requirements, consult with an agent able to obtain insurance coverage from any company. Check your telephone directory for Independent Insurance Agents Association (IIAA) or Professional Insurance Agents (PIA), listed under Insurance.

It is safe to assume that your efforts have been rewarded, and your creative works are fully protected. As an exhibiting artist, your main concerns center around conditions in and out of your residence, in particular regarding those works scheduled on your PAP.

In-Home Protection

A copy of the itemized fine arts list is attached to your policy for easy reference and the original is retained by the insurance company. In the event of a catastrophe, the floater will guarantee reimbursement for the limit of liability for each work destroyed, provided you file the claim within sixty days after the loss. You must sign a sworn proof of loss, stating the facts and amount of loss. You also agree to be examined under oath and to produce witnesses to verify your loss, if necessary. You will produce, when and if requested, the remains of the damaged property and records to verify the claim and the amount. If your work or works are not completely destroyed and repairable to the original condition, the policy will cover you for that amount. This procedure and ultimate coverage depends in part on certain inclusions and special exclusions as stated in the policy. How does the coverage work?

1. A fire in the corner of your studio consumes two oil paintings valued at $1,500 which are listed on your personal articles schedule.
2. A representative from your insurance company investigates your claim.
3. You sign a proof of loss, providing facts, value of your works as listed under limit of liability, and you and your spouse swear under oath to the events.
4. You are awarded $1,500 which now reduces your original $10,000 coverage to $8,500. You elect to pay a reduced premium for $8,500 or replace the lost works with two oil paintings by submitting their description and value in writing to arrive at $10,000 to retain your original coverage.

In-Transport Protection

Your fine arts floater allows you to ship, with full property coverage, only those works listed on the schedule. It is advisable to submit in writing to your insurance agent the title, price, where the work is being shipped, length of stay, and approximate date of return. Keep a copy of your letter.

As of June 1, 1984 State Farm Insurance provides property coverage for losses caused by breakage under any circumstances, while in transit; fire, lightning, aircraft, theft, windstorm, earthquake, flood, explosion, malicious damage, or collision, derailment or overturn of any conveyance. This recent reversal from an exclusion to an inclusion clause is of immeasurable benefit when your work is shipped. However—*You agree that the covered property will be packed and unpacked by competent packers*. There can be no quarrel with this statement inasmuch as this requirement is imposed by sponsoring organizations and commercial shippers as well.

If and when there is a loss or damage, the insurance provided by a commercial carrier will be deducted from the coverage amount limits under your floater. For instance, UPS, which provides $100 free insurance, will honor that amount if your work is lost or damaged. But your insurance company will deduct the $100 from the amount it pays you.

There is another condition. If you ship a set of three statues and two are destroyed beyond repair, you'll be paid for the face value of the set if you surrender the remaining statue.

Based on these two conditions, no additional insurance is needed once your works are covered by the fine arts floater. But you must inform your insurance agent in writing, as previously mentioned, that your work is being shipped.

Protection While on Exhibition

Coverage applies if your works are exhibited within the

United States and Canada and are included on your personal articles schedule. This is a particularly worthwhile benefit since most sponsoring organizations cannot afford to insure a valuable exhibition of artworks.

By contrast, the Clark Arts Center Gallery of Rockford College, in Rockford, Illinois, sponsors of the "Rockford International" print and drawing Biennale '85, makes a sincere effort to provide at least some form of insurance for participating artists:—*Works accepted by the juror, after the final judging, will be insured for the duration of the show. Any other insurance is the responsibility of the artist.*

The American Watercolor Society will insure only works accepted for its annual traveling exhibition, limited to $1,000 per painting. Paintings sold while on tour are fully insured. This is quite generous of AWS, considering that fifty works will be shipped, unpacked, exhibited, repacked, and shipped to ten different locations around the country.

The DeLand Museum, sponsors of Southeastern Watercolorists II, states: *Accepted entries will be fully protected by modern security measures and full insurance.*

The North American Sculpture Exhibition will cover each work for full value while on its premises, with a $100 deductible provision. In the event of a $500 claim, you will receive $400.

These examples are exceptions to the rule. Unless you provide some form of security for your works, they are vulnerable to damage without recourse. Accidents can happen.

Liability

What is the meaning of this word that often sends individuals, businesses, and industry scurrying for stricter interpretation by insurance companies and attorneys? Definition: li-a-bil-i-ty n. the state of being liable; responsibility; obligation.

How it applies to your dealings with the sponsoring organization when you actively participate in an exhibition is related to the conditions both parties agree to. Does an organization accept responsibility for your work while on its premises? The answer appears contradictory in that it will assume responsibility *within restricted limits but not to the extent of liability*. Some organizations avoid the possibility of liability with insurance coverage. The majority are not financially able to accept responsibility. If you have read these prospectuses with care, it becomes immediately apparent that acceptance of responsibility is explicitly denied. You must either agree with the statement's meaning or render yourself ineligible.

The Hudson River Museum states—*The Museum and the Hudson River Contemporary Artists will not assume responsibility for loss or damage, whether arising from negligence or otherwise to accepted works. Entries will be handled with utmost care.*

When Hudson River Museum includes the phrase, "*. . . arising from negligence or otherwise*," it is saying that in spite of a deep regard for your work, unavoidable accidents can happen.

San Diego Watercolor Society goes one step further in saying that—*Neither the San Diego Watercolor Society nor the Gallery owners nor any receiving or leasing agent will be responsible for loss or damage to any work of art submitted to this exhibition. Each individual artist should carry his own insurance for shipping and/or during the exhibition. Submitting a work of art to this exhibition shall imply an agreement on the part of the artist to the conditions set forth above.*

The society, typical of so many that mount exhibitions on outside premises and which use a receiving agent to uncrate and deliver works, is required to protect both the exhibition site, Grossmont College Art Gallery and its agent, Fragile Handle with Care of San Diego. Without their inclusion, the gallery and the agent could legally be liable for damage or loss. This clause is all inclusive and effectively conceived.

Allied Artists of America, Inc. states in part: *Experienced attendants will handle the works of art. Please take proper precautions in fastening pictures in frames and attaching labels.*

How does this statement differ from the others? "*Please take proper precautions in fastening pictures in frames . . . ,*" is a clue to problems faced by many organizations. What Allied actually implies is that prevention of damage is a mutual responsibility. A work that is carelessly assembled may withstand the rigors of shipment when solidly cushioned and confined in a crate, but will it resist the many handlings it goes through during the course of an exhibition?

You may wonder why some organizations fail to include a disclaimer of liability. The reason for such negligence is difficult to answer since its exclusion is frought with implications. Would you have the legal right to seek restitution for damage or loss? The answer is yes, but whether a court of law would decide in your favor depends on the extent, nature, and cause of the occurrence. The cost of seeking counsel may not justify the action.

I am not suggesting that you abdicate your legal rights. My advice is that in the event of loss or damage, negotiate directly with the sponsoring organization. If this fails, then seek counsel. A simple resolution to the problem of securing effective protection is insurance, not litigation.

After almost thirty years of exhibiting competitively, not one of my works was seriously damaged or lost. My frames have suffered the normal scars inflicted in delivering and handling. My experiences are not a guarantee that some unfortunate accident may not happen to one of your works. But I cite them to dramatize the potential of damage as being limited. Still, what *can* you do to protect your works?

1. Avoid materials susceptible to damage
2. Pack shipped works with adequate protection
3. Insure your works

Copyright Infringement

In the review of copyright and its features that protect against infringement of one's rights, we realize that some prospectuses may deny you access to this legal right. How is this possible? Under stated conditions, infringement is possible (and valid from every standpoint) when wholly dependent upon mutual agreement. Organizations, cognizant of your rights and forced by lack of funds, will include a waiver of liability in the prospectus. Participation in the exhibition hinges on your acceptance of this condition.

Southeastern Watercolorists II states—*Submission of entries constitutes an agreement between the artist and the Museum to all conditions in this application, including permission to reproduce works in the exhibit catalog, press and other places.*

"*Other places*," albeit a somewhat nebulous statement, does not imply indiscriminate and wholesale use of reproduction rights for gain but is meant to seize alternative and available publicity opportunities.

The Cooperstown Art Association's prospectus includes a statement that succinctly expresses its intentions—*The Association reserves the right to photograph works in the exhibition for publicity purposes.*

Brush and Palette Club, Western Colorado Center for the Arts states that—*Entering artists agree to abide by the rules of the show and give permission to photograph or reproduce any entry for publicity purposes unless otherwise stated.*

The Brush and Palette Club is wisely, and legally, advising you of your right of refusal of reproduction of your work. A more important consideration is that acceptance is not contingent on waiving this right, provided a written refusal is submitted.

The Iron Horse Festival Art Show and the National Watercolor Society go one step further. Iron Horse states in part: *Iron Horse Festival has my permission to photo-*

graph my work for publicity purposes. . . . Room is provided for your signature in acceptance of the condition, making this a perfectly legal agreement. Whereas the National Watercolor Society states—*Permission to reproduce entries in the catalog or for publicity purposes is assumed unless noted on the entry form.* In this instance your options are left open.

These representative examples of "waiver" comply with the letter of the copyright law. By contrast, does the exclusion of such disclaimer:

a. Refute the intent of the law?
b. Express ignorance of the law?
c. Depict negligence?
d. Imply no intention to photograph or reproduce works of art?

Whatever the answer, your rights remain inviolate, and action on your part is subject to the extent of infringement. However, disclaimer or not, refusing permission under any circumstance denies you valuable publicity and exposure. Indeed, would you refuse permission to have a reproduction of your prize winning entry included in a handsomely printed catalog, the local newspaper, or periodical? You should use reasonable judgment in making such decisions.

Many years ago, before the revised copyright statute took effect, my medal-winning watercolor was reproduced in black and white on the cover of a trade art magazine without my knowledge. In spite of the infringement I weighed the pros and cons of the issue and let the matter stand in consideration of the incalculable measure of residual benefits. Letters from various parts of the country and congratulatory messages from colleagues and friends gave me an emotional lift. A major benefit included a full-color reproduction on the cover of a book of award-winning watercolors plus a full page with an autobiographical review.

Questions

Q. *Can you tell me why I was refused special insurance for my paintings even though the company in question insures me for everything else?*

A. Not all insurance companies provide this service. In some cases the extent of risk, correlated to the low premium necessary to remain competitive, prohibits the writing of such policies.

Q. *Is it fair to keep an entry fee if your work is rejected?*

A. Consider the fee a form of subsidy to support the organization, or as an appraisal charge of your work, or as remuneration for the expenses and physical effort in mounting an exhibition, or as assurance that emerging artists to follow will support your entry when you move onward to bigger challenges.

Q. *Why do entry fees vary so much?*

A. A good question! It is no surprise that the most attractive and prestigious exhibiting opportunities often impose a lesser fee than others. This paradox is answerable by a simple economics question—Is it wiser to sell 2,000 raffle tickets at $10 each with excellent potential for rewards, or 800 at $25 each? The answer is a matter of judgment, cultural involvement, and policy by the organization. If the entry fee becomes a financial burden, select those opportunities which demand less expense. You can arrange a substantial exhibition schedule within your own state.

Conclusion

Competitive exhibitions are a gamble that pits works against works for financial rewards, prestige, and exposure. That participation becomes addictive. But without guidelines to prepare the artist his chances of success are limited. Where to show, and when, are prime considerations. This understanding creates the potential for success on various levels of exhibiting from the local artist's group through the commercial/industrial level.

Each level of competition has different standards for creative competency. Prestigious shows attract the greatest number of quality entries and offer the stiffest competition. This provides a clue to dictate one's direction: the emerging artist will find more exposure and fulfillment in participating at levels commensurate with his ability. With creative development and a growing understanding of the exhibition process, higher rungs of the competitive system become less formidable. These new experiences in various environments offer the opportunity to participate in the governing process of an organization. Such added knowledge does not in itself enhance the chances of success in the exhibition process but provides a greater understanding of the mechanics of preparing for any level of competition. This knowledge minimizes the potential for errors that plague artists.

Access to information about exhibition opportunities is as readily available as newspapers, art magazines, the county art council, etc.

The prospectus—a document that spells out the responsibilities of both the artist and the sponsoring organization—is more involved than it appears. A step-by-step analysis of those provisions common to most prospectuses, and others that are peculiar only to some organizations, concludes that these documents constitute binding agreements between participants. Also prospectuses, although similar in content, are distinctly different and demand careful reading.

Provisions in a prospectus that dictate limitations for

entry are pertinent to eligibility for acceptance. For instance, regular glass, allowable in one year, is not necessarily allowable in subsequent years, and failing to abide by a newly instituted provision is a sure-fire reason for automatic rejection.

Another often overlooked rule is the limitation imposed on the size of works. Other provisions are eligible media, delivery and return of works, entry fees, insurance and liability, and other restrictions that vary from one organization to another. Such provisions are meant to define, in specific terms, the responsibilities of the entrant and are not meant to be either interpreted or challenged.

However, adherence to these provisions does not imply a blind capitulation to demands that seem either excessive or unreasonable. Options are still available to the artist. He may question (either by phone or in writing) the meaning of an unclear rule and expect a reasonable answer, or he may by-pass the exhibition opportunity.

The introduction of slide submissions in lieu of actual work has become an apparent advantage that minimizes the artist's expense and time involvement. Although there are sponsoring organizations which still demand the delivery of actual works (without prejudging by slides), the future holds little hope for this method except for local and state shows.

The artist needs to either find costly professional help for shooting slides or to invest in the necessary photographic equipment and do it himself. The cost of camera equipment need not be prohibitive and there's no mystery to shooting slides. Even artists with limited camera experience can learn to shoot acceptable slides. With a period of trial and error, a measure of experimentation with various types of film (both indoor and outdoor), and an understanding of various film processing options, the process becomes less formidable. This is also true of black-and-white prints needed for three-dimensional works.

However we view this new development in the submission process, it cannot be ignored if we expect to expand our exhibition horizons. Keep in mind that until the advent of this procedure, the cost of shipping a piece of work, which might be rejected by a jury, questioned the viability of the art competition system. Now only accepted works need to be shipped.

Experience has shown that a continuous involvement in the art competition process demands a method of record keeping to provide not only accurate data but to maintain control of creative activity.

An accurate exhibition schedule is indispensable in preventing a repeat submission of a work that renders it ineligible for consideration. You cannot verify the completion date of a work without a production record as a reference source. This is true of all record-keeping procedures that minimize the search for answers for both art works and slides.

The completion of a creative exercise always faces the inevitable question—what to do to enhance the image. Since few exhibitions permit works submitted to be unframed, many artists prefer easy solutions to the problem in spite of inner stirrings to the contrary. There are several ways to fabricate your own frames rather than contracting a professional to do the work.

Framing is mcant to be protective as well as aesthetically pleasing. Wood moldings versus metal sections and glass versus synthetics should be compared and evaluated as to advantages and disadvantages of each, keeping in mind that glass is becoming more and more prohibited in competitive exhibitions.

There are several shipping methods for both two-dimensional and three-dimensional works, depending on restrictions imposed by the prospectus and by shipping companies. Carrier restrictions regarding size of works supersede those imposed by the sponsoring organization.

Packing materials are available from several sources, free for the asking or at a reasonable cost. The effort placed in the protection of works of art, whethe^r in local or long distance shipping must be at least equal to the creative effort.

The very existence of the competitive system depends on entry fees as a form of support by the artist. Whether or not the artist receives a fair chance for his investment is not the question since it has been decided that the exhibition process is a gamble at best.

Another important aspect of exhibiting is insurance protection for artworks while at home, in transit, and while on someone else's premises. This seems particularly crucial since art organizations usually fail to assume responsibility for loss or damage.

You need also to remember that:

1. Reputable art organizations are primarily nonprofit in structure, governed by members of the board of directors who in turn must abide by organizational by-laws. Decisions are not made arbitrarily but after due deliberation and with the interests in mind of its general membership and the cultural community.

2. There is a periodic re-evaluation by organization committees of provisions found in the prospectus to clarify their meaning to benefit the exhibiting artist (the slide submission being a case in point).

3. The sponsoring organization does everything in its power to proliferate its cultural aims and strives to engender the respect and interest of the exhibiting artist to participate in its competitive exhibitions. It needs you to survive.

On the other hand, there is the artist looking for exposure to enhance his reputation. What voice does he have in the exhibition system? From a competitive standpoint—very little. The artist's responsibility is to protect his own interests. He needs to chart a reasonable course and learn to realize that the competitive system provides unlimited opportunities for exposure and gain.

Index